ROUSSEAU AND MARX

ROUSSEAU AND MARX

and other writings

by

Galvano della Volpe

translated and introduced by John Fraser

HUMANITIES PRESS
Atlantic Highlands, N.J.

Humanities Press Inc.
Atlantic Highlands, N.J.

This edition published by Humanities Press Inc., 1979

First published in Italian as *Rousseau e Marx* by
Editori Riuniti, Rome 1964

English edition first published 1978
© Lawrence and Wishart Ltd, London

Printed and bound in Great Britain at
The Camelot Press Ltd, Southampton

CONTENTS

FOR A MATERIALIST METHODOLOGY OF
ECONOMICS AND OF THE MORAL DISCIPLINES
IN GENERAL
(On Marx's methodological writings from 1843 to 1859)

TRANSLATOR'S INTRODUCTION

Galvano della Volpe (1895–1968) was the most influential and original post-war Italian Marxist philosopher, though his work is still largely unknown in the English-speaking world. The essays which make up *Rousseau and Marx* have their origins in the 1940s, a period in which della Volpe moved rapidly from a Rousseauan to a Marxist position. They now stand as a major contribution to the current debate on the continuity and renewal of direct, Rousseauan democracy and Kantian legal-constitutional guarantees in a 'State of socialist legality'.[1]

Allusive and compressed, the texts present formidable difficulties to the reader. The constant re-working of the balance between the Rousseauan and Kantian elements of socialist democracy (its 'two souls') demands alertness to shifts of stress and interpretation. While della Volpe regarded himself as consistently faithful to the heritage and political philosophy of Lenin and to Marx's critique of the liberal, representative state, he was alive to the contemporary implications of his discussion and its changing emphases. Indeed, between the first and third editions of *Rousseau and Marx* (1957–62) he was acting as a major philosophical spokesman for the Italian Communist Party, particularly through his membership of the editorial board of the Party's theoretical journal, *Società*.[2]

The reader is at once struck by the vehement rejection by della Volpe of idealism, and by his opposition to the contamination of Marxism by historicist idealism – a deep-rooted tendency in Italian Marxism. The revival of idealist philosophy at the end of the last century had left a deep imprint on Italian Marxist theory. The

Southern Hegelians' critique of the imperfect national unity achieved by the Risorgimento gave Italian Hegelianism an explicitly political orientation. However, in the next generation, Gentile's 'activist' philosophy associated idealism with fascism, and Croce's 'absolute historicism' allowed his liberal opposition to fascism to become an impotent detachment from politics. To della Volpe, this seemingly divided political tradition in Italian idealism rested, in the last resort, on the *unity* of idealism's philosophical, cultural and *bourgeois* universe.

The exclusion of Communists from the government in 1947 had made discussion of the nature of the bourgeois-democratic state immediately relevant to the political strategy of the Party in the light of Togliatti's decision to continue to accept the constitutional road for achieving power. The discussion became more intense in the years following the death of Stalin, when the Party faced a challenge to its virtual monopoly in determining the political loyalties of the Marxist 'schools' which coexisted and flourished in the post-war years within its sphere of influence. The proliferation of groups of militants and intellectuals outside the Party in the 1960s further concentrated attention on the political implications of Marxist studies of the state.[3]

By 1956, when the compilation of *Rousseau and Marx* was first undertaken, della Volpe was a veteran of the post-war struggle against idealism. Many intellectuals had by then begun to re-examine critically the relation between 'culture' (as defined by idealist philosophy), and politics. The tendency among left intellectuals to withdraw from politics following the Twentieth Congress of the Soviet Party was soon reversed by the experience of the repressive Tambroni government, and the peak and decline of Italian neocapitalism. The four editions of *Rousseau and Marx*, published between 1957 and 1964, appeared at a time of heightened political and philosophical activity on the left. They coincided with a major reassessment of the Soviet political system. They expressed the revaluation of the relation between Marxist studies and political commitment. They bore directly on the analysis by left-wing intellectuals of their own relation to demands for liberty and equality in liberal-bourgeois, and in socialist, states. The topicality of these issues gave the book, then as now, a significance beyond merely textual examination of Marx's (and Engels's) underlying, 'unconscious' debt to Rousseau.

Della Volpe had had the typical career of an obscure, conforming academic under fascism. He had, however, early broken intellectual ties with Gentile and Croce. He had also criticized the Hegelian dialectic as a theological, degenerate form of Kant's problematic. His major work in the 1930s was a study of Hume, and his Marxism (in 1944–6) was reached by way of the Rousseau of the *Discourse* on inequality. His was a long and individual search for a rational materialism consonant both with the concrete, empirical world of activity, human labour, and with modern scientific logic. This had made him a unique, as well as an isolated and virtually unknown, figure among post-war Party intellectuals. He attempted, using textual rather than sociological or historical analyses, to expound the *system* of Marxism and its kinship with modern scientific and philosophical logic. Thus, the ethics and politics form part of a methodological unity provided by Marx's discovery of a scientific basis for the moral disciplines. This concentration on science, on textual analysis and, in *Rousseau and Marx*, the relation between Enlightenment rationalism and the experience of the proletarian state, clearly distinguished della Volpe's problematic from that of Gramsci.

Della Volpe in short rejects the historicist tradition in Italian Marxist thought, while not denying Marx a scientific theory of history. He was also opposed to the anti-Leninist stance of revisionist theorists such as Rodolfo Mondolfo – incidentally, a former teacher of della Volpe. He thus combines elements of historical continuity with the search for fresh, original readings of classical theory, enlightened by a scientific, experimental attitude to received ideas. *Rousseau and Marx* is not a hybrid, nor an eclectic, work. Its arguments are derived from close study of the theories of the individual, the person, in Rousseau and Kant, and an evaluation of what is alive in these writers' conceptions of political freedom and equality. Della Volpe's interpretation of the transmission and renewal of these ideas in Marx, Engels and Lenin makes the essays a contentious but basic contribution to the discussion of the relation of modern bourgeois democracy to socialist democracy.

For the most part, standard English translations of citations in the text have been used. In some instances, della Volpe quoted in the language of the original, or made his own translations, in order to establish his arguments more firmly. Where the force of these arguments would be lessened by citing the familiar English versions, I have made my own. Della Volpe's emphases are retained throughout, and his footnotes and references expanded and corrected where necessary. Sentences and paragraphs have been divided, and explanatory notes added. The result is a compromise which tries to retain the denseness and rigour of the original while providing the English-speaking reader with a more readily accessible text and bibliographic references.

The text is translated from the revised, final edition of 1964,* now reprinted in *Rousseau e Marx e altri saggi di critica materialistica* in the collected works (*Opere*) definitively edited by Ignazio Ambrogio (Rome: Editori Riuniti, 1973, vol. 5). Most of the textual variations included in Ambrogio's edition have been left out in this translation. The present edition also omits the 'Five Fragments on Ethics', the 'Note on Logical Positivism', 'Aristotle, 1955', 'The Dialectic without Idealism' and the 'Summary Outline of Method'. The 'Fragments' are slight, occasional pieces, and the other essays omitted are scarcely

---

* Dates of the first publication of the individual essays are given on the Contents' page in this English edition.

comprehensible to the reader unfamiliar with della Volpe's '*logic as positive* (historical) *science*' (in *Opere*, vol. 6).

NOTES

1. Della Volpe's complete work is available in the six-volume *Opere* (Rome: Editori Riuniti, 1972–3.) See, too, my *Introduction to the Thought of Galvano della Volpe* (London: Lawrence and Wishart, 1977). Della Volpe's theory of the state is discussed in Danilo Zolo, *La teoria comunista dell'estinzione dello stato* (Bari: De Donato, 1974), in Emilio Agazzi, 'Significato e limiti del dellavolpismo nella storia del marxismo italiano' (Milan: Istituto Feltrinelli, 1974 [cyclostyled]), and Riccardo Guastini and Renato Levrero, 'Garantismo e programmazione democratica', *Classe* 3, 1970.

2. Cf. Lucio Colletti, 'A political and philosophical interview', *New Left Review*, no. 86 (July–August 1974).

3. See, for example, Nicola Badaloni, *Il marxismo italiano degli anni sessanta*, in the volume of that title (Rome: Editori Riuniti-Istituto Gramsci, 1972), Giacomo Marramao, *Marxismo e revisionismo in Italia* (Bari: De Donato, 1971), and Franco Cassano (ed.), *Marxismo e filosofia in Italia 1958–71* (Bari: De Donato, 1973).

ROUSSEAU AND MARX

To the students of the
ISTITUTO GRAMSCI

PREFACE TO THE FOURTH EDITION

The novelty of this fourth edition lies in the four appendices added to the essay whose title is that of the book, and in some more than merely formal revisions, made primarily to that essay. To start with the latter, we draw attention, for the convenience of the reader, to the following pages (for comparison with the corresponding pages in the third edition): pp. 34, 36, 54, 65, 77, 83, 92–3, 97, 99, 104 and later pp. 193, 196, 200–01. These revisions are incorporated in the forthcoming French edition by Maspero of Paris,[1] as they are intended to perfect the method of *historical-dialectical analysis* pursued by the author, here chiefly applied to problems of political philosophy.

As for the appendices, the first, and most important in the author's judgement, is a return to the question of socialist legality (with some repetition, inevitable and perhaps useful in material of this kind). For bourgeois philosophy, this fundamental question is a kind of *lucus a non lucendi* (notwithstanding the unconventional demand made, for instance, by Norberto Bobbio, 'that one should begin to understand law no longer as a bourgeois phenomenon, but as a system of technical norms which can be employed as much by proletarians as by bourgeois to pursue certain aims common to them both, insofar as both are social beings').[2] The question is thus of little interest to Marxists, at least judging by recent, otherwise valuable, studies of materialist political philosophy, perhaps for the reason that, indeed, the subject is not to be found among the 'topics' of classical Marxism.[3] The second appendix attempts to set forth the meaning of the real historical turning-point represented by the radical, democratic humanism of Jean-Jacques, as against the liberal humanism of Montesquieu and the bourgeois-conservative humanism, and corresponding social scepticism, of Voltaire. The third is intended to fix the position (without preconceptions) of the 'fate' of Rousseau at the hands of the founders of scientific socialism and those who continue their work in the Soviet Union. The fourth, with a scientific examination of the present Italian constitution, attempts to draw the *practical* conclusions which concern democratic Communists. These pieces, republished here with minor changes as appendices to the first (philosophico-political) essay of the collection, appeared in *Il Contemporaneo*, 53, October 1962 (the second), *Critica marxista*, 2 March–April 1963 (the third) *Mondo nuovo*, 22 April 1962 (the fourth), and *Critica marxista*, 1 January 1964 (the first, which will appear in English in the forthcoming miscellany *Socialist Humanism* edited by Erich Fromm, published by Doubleday, New York).[4]

Messina, the University, 10 January 1964

NOTES

1. Published instead as *Rousseau et autres essais de critique matérialiste*, edited and translated by Robert Paris (Paris: Grasset, 1974).
2. Norberto Bobbio, *Politica e cultura* (Turin: Einaudi, 1955) (1974 edn, p. 156). (Bobbio, a philosopher at the University of Turin, is a critic of the PCI from the non-communist left.)
3. A reference to Aristotle's *Topica*.
4. Published in 1965.

NOTE TO THE READER (1961)

The essay which gives its title to the volume (and has especially earned it some success) has been extensively reworked, and this, its third edition, replaces also the German version of the first edition (in the *Deutsche Zeitschrift für Philosophie*, East Berlin, 1961, no. 6). In the present form of publication of that essay are thus brought together the results of a period of research into political philosophy from 1943 to the present (and cf. the 'Author's note' which prefaces the first edition).[1] The last but one of the 'Clarifications' which complete the essay is the revised Italian text of an article written for the special number of the review *Europe* (November–December 1961), dedicated to Rousseau.

The other essay, *For a materialist methodology of economics and of the moral disciplines in general*, which with the above constitutes the main part of the volume, is unchanged, except for the explanatory subtitles now added in brackets to each part. This essay corresponds faithfully to the German version (in the *Zeitschrift*, op. cit., 1958, no. 5).

Messina, the University, 21 December 1961

NOTE

1. Reprinted in *Opere*, op. cit., pp. 480–1.

INTRODUCTION

Here, the case is made for the following fundamental historico-systematic thesis: that from now on, the social-democratic interpretation of the Rousseauan message on liberty and human personality, made from a natural-law perspective (witness, for example, Rodolfo Mondolfo),[1] belongs to the past. There it joins the superficial, commonplace view of Rousseau as the utopian philosopher of the 'little States' and the radical petty bourgeoisie, peddler of 'cures' like the levelling of classes so that there will be neither rich nor poor. This Rousseau of the 'egalitarians', in the style of Babeuf, etc., was the only Rousseau, it seems, known to Vyshinsky.[2] In the social-democratic interpretation, the historical connection of Rousseau with socialism would lie in the formal, anachronistic, reduction of the case for socialism to the *Declaration of the Rights of Man and Citizen*, and of the socialist demand to a perfunctory appendix of it. We forget that however much a Rousseauan (natural law) spirit infuses the *Declaration*, this is historically exhausted by the bourgeois revolution.

On the contrary, rather, the living substance of the Rousseauan message on (egalitarian) liberty must be seen in the universal (democratic) demand for personal 'merit';[3] that is, the need for the (social) recognition of *every* human individual, with his special merits and requirements. The *proportional* division of the product of labour in communist society among all the ('different') individuals, expressed theoretically by Marx in the *Critique of the Gotha Programme* and by Lenin in *State and Revolution*, is itself destined only to represent the historical *fulfilment* of the Rousseauan demand for personal merit,[4] in fact, in the basic aspect of the economic life of the individual. In short, the nature of the historical connection between Rousseau and socialism, and of the continuation of the genuine, Rousseauan, *egalitarian problematic* in scientific socialism is obvious only in these terms. Thus, not only does the meaning of the relation between democracy and socialism necessarily become clear, but so too does the whole general question of the complex significance of the term 'modern democracy'.

The many implications of the basic argument, which are dealt with below, derive from the different, relative historical and theoretical scope of the *Discourse on Inequality* and the *Social Contract* as regards the following problems: (a) the modalities and meaning of the renewal of the bourgeois-democratic heritage under conditions of democratic-socialist legality, and the corresponding structure of the socialist state (with its democratic centralism); (b) the meaning of the 'withering away of the state'; and, (c) the nature of communist society.

NOTES

1. Rodolfo Mondolfo (1877–1958) was a reformist socialist, influential as a follower of the idealist interpretation of Marx (cf. Giacomo Marramao, *Marxismo e revisionismo in Italia* (Bari: De Donato, 1971) and the Introduction by N. Bobbio to Mondolfo's essays *Umanismo di Marx* (Turin: Einaudi, 1968)). He was della Volpe's teacher, and wrote on Marx (1919) and Engels (1912).
2. A. Ya. Vyshinsky (1883–1954). Procurator of the USSR, 1935–9, and Minister for Foreign Affairs, 1949–53, he was also Director of the Institute of Law, Soviet Academy of Sciences, 1937–41.
3. This has the sense of 'services' as well as 'qualities' and 'achievements'.
4. i.e. the recognition of personal merit or worth.

I

CRITIQUE OF ROUSSEAU'S ABSTRACT MAN

And for a society based upon the production of commodities, in which the producers in general enter into social relations with one another by treating their products as *commodities* and *values*, whereby they reduce their individual private labour to the *standard* of *homogeneous human labour* – for such a society, *Christianity* with its *cultus* of abstract man, more especially in its protestant developments, Protestantism, Deism, etc., is the most fitting *form of religion.*[1]*

This sphere that we are deserting, within whose boundaries the sale and purchase of labour-power goes on, is in fact a very *Eden of the innate rights of man.*[2]

1

For Rousseau, the spiritual father of modern democracy, 'moral consciousness' consists in the 'sentiment of humanity' or humanitarian love. 'The love of men', he says, 'derived from *love of oneself* [not to be confused with narcissistic 'self love'], is the principle of human justice.'[3] Again, 'it is from the moral system formed by this *double relation* with *oneself* and *one's fellows* that the impulse of *conscience* is born', and which 'makes man like God'.[4] The explanation of this double relation which goes to make up conscience is that since 'love for the *Author* of one's own being [. . .] is *confused* with this same love of oneself',[5] in turn love of oneself and love of one's fellow beings are *confused* or coincide. This is a double relation, derived from the fundamental relation of union (love) of each one of us with God, the *transcendent universal*, in which the following fact is confirmed and made precise: that it is out of love of God that one should love one's neighbour, that is, one's

* See notes at the end of each section.

fellow-being, as *oneself*. This is no less (and also no more) than *religious egotism*, only in that sense *moral*, as presented in the famous Rousseauan statement that 'when the power of an *expansive* soul identifies me with my fellow-being, and I feel myself, so to speak, in him, it is so as not to suffer that I wish him not to suffer, and am concerned for him *out of love for myself*'.[6]

The person, or individual-value, in a practical sense is built round this egotism *sui generis*. The person as *original*, or *a priori*, *pre-social* or *pre-historical*, is itself a person as arbitrary, dogmatic unity of the individual or particular with a universal which *absolutely transcends history*, instead of being a unity with the historical universal of the human species. Hence one understands precisely how Rousseau could state right away that 'the fullest idea I can form of Providence is that every material being should be ordered in the best possible way *in relation to the whole*, and every intelligent, feeling being in the best possible way *in relation to himself*'. So, 'I tell you, in the name of God, that it is the part which is *greater than the whole*',[7] and hence he can fully accept the *paradox of abstract, Christian individualism*. This paradox means that for the human individual the law of the relation of the singular to the whole, of the individual to the species, *is not valid*. This calls for comparison with its echo in Kierkegaard's 'mankind has the peculiarity that precisely because the individual is created in the *image of God*, the *singular is higher than the species*'.[8]

Thus one can understand the full, accurate, moral significance of the famous formulae of the '*natural* man' and of the '*return to nature*'. Here is the *a priori*, Platonic-Christian basis, *romantic* before its time, of Rousseau's individualism, which has his Savoyard vicar say: 'Too often reason deceives us [. . .], but *conscience* [that is, the innate *sentiment* of *love of oneself* which is *love of one's neighbour*, being also *love of God*] never deceives: he who follows it, obeys *nature* [. . .]. Let us turn back *into ourselves*.'[9] This is the individualist Rousseau who, confronting the problem of political society which is typically that of the *historical species of man*, warns that 'everything depends on *not destroying the natural man* in adapting him to *society*'.[10] However, at this stage one understands also the enormous difficulty placed before the *political* Rousseau by these same general ethical and metaphysical premises. These are the dogmatic axiom of the *natural man*, and of the *individual* – free and independent in the sense that hereby is conferred his original *a priori conscience*. Hence too there arises the unavoidable corollary that in becoming socio-political, the natural man retrieves his specific integrity as an *original person* or individual endowed with *a priori* value at the expense of his likeness to God: at the expense, that is, of his union with the transcendent, meta-historical universal which is God.

This is a difficulty already present in the famous formula of the 'fundamental problem', whose solution should be found in the 'social contract'. This is a formula in which is set forth the need to 'find a form of *association* which can *defend* and *protect* with all its *common strength* the *person* and *goods* of each member [that is, which will safeguard the right of property and all the other associated "natural", pure, and rational rights, or the *absolute* private claims of the original, pre-social person, who is the natural man], and by means of which each, uniting himself with all, still obeys only himself and *stays free as before*'.[11] Rousseau's difficulty therefore, is that of having to base political society, or the temporal, historical organism which it is, on elements as refractory as the original, pre-social, absolute and 'imprescriptible' rights of natural man. This natural man is the individual as individual-value or person, but has rights derived from a union with a universal or species transcending history, by means of a kind of extra-temporal, extra-historical, investiture – instead of through union with his own *historical species*, the human.

It is true that the attempt to resolve this major difficulty by a clause in the 'contract' contributed historically to the realization of *humanitarian* equality of the Christian type –

in the area of 'civil' or political law. The clause is the one which speaks of the 'complete alienation of every member with all his [natural, original] rights to the community *as a whole*', through which 'each giving himself to *all* gives himself to *no-one*'.[12] To resolve the difficulty, Rousseau substituted the 'law' as expression of the 'general will' issuing from the 'contract' for the 'ordinances', 'letters patent' and 'edicts' of the monarch. This was the *political* equality instituted by the French Revolution. From this was derived the emancipation – political – of the 'common' man. However, it is also true that with the 'general will' constituting the new 'body politic',[13] it is still necessary to conclude that the equality instituted by and for such a body politic can only be justified as that type of equality which *religious egotism* permits. The 'general will' has its ideological foundation in 'moral conscience' as 'sentiment of humanity' or humanitarian love, which in turn is nothing more than that religious *egotism* described above, in which traditional Christian individualism is absorbed.

Such is the equality-inequality which results from understanding *equality as a function of liberty*, but *not also vice versa*. Not also vice versa precisely because the *person*, with whom *liberty* is identified, is that abstract, solitary, pre-social, pre-historical individual, the Christian *original person*, beginning and end of that *egotism* of *humanitarian love* (as a typical lay version of *caritas*).

Consequently, equality as here described can be no more than an extrinsic, *formal*, abstract and *juridical* equality, in that it is only the 'legal' or 'artificial' translation of 'natural' claims and rights. In short, it is a *legitimation* of an original, extra-historical, mythical liberty or independence. It cannot be that intrinsic, *substantial*, real equality which is the *social* equality demanded by the historical, real act of *communal life* which characterizes the concrete human being not separated from his species. Only this real equality carries with it a liberty which is real because *social*, and which being thus liberty in and for the *community*, is truly the liberty of *all*.

Thus one comes to understand the disequilibrium of liberty and justice, or equality, which undermines *this* Rousseauan political society and, indirectly, 'bourgeois democracy'. Rousseau wanted to emancipate the 'people' by freeing the 'roturier' (commoner) or plebeian, in whom he saw the chief incarnation of his type of common 'man', the artisan, the small peasant farmer – the small and middle bourgeois, in short. Hence, it fell to him to set out the ideal terms for the emancipation not of the people as a *whole*, nor simply of the *people*, but only of the *bourgeoisie*, the whole bourgeoisie, large and small, a single class. Precisely by following from the ideological standpoint his basic conception of the human individual as individual-value, or person, we reach that *natural man* whose *absoluteness* or original independence and subsequent 'free enterprise' gives him his specific characteristic – concretely, that of *common-bourgeois man*.

It will already be seen that the *proletarian* must be excluded from this ideological framework. The proletarian is *common* man specifically as *worker*, and as such man in the *mass*, or *social* man *par excellence*, through whom the *organic* and *ordering* nature of *labour* is demonstrated in the highest degree.

Finishing with *this* Rousseau, it seems clear that the ideological limits of his democracy can be summed up in the particular deficiency of the principle of the 'sentiment of humanity' or of *humanitarianism*, and of the implicit view of man as 'natural man', or *a priori man, original person*, as it were. Here is the whole Rousseauan ideological justification of a society divided into classes, and hence still cleft by inequalities – which he could not see. For, if a class society generally entails a conception of *rights* which are for the most part *expanded privileges*, how can it be denied that those rights are destined to be privileges insofar as they are intended to be *deduced* as such from the *original dignity* of a human individual thus abstracted from the historical society of his species?

One thinks of the *absoluteness*, abstractness, and also the *inhumanity* which marks the traditional, bourgeois right of 'property', justified in terms of natural law, in a Rousseauan manner, by an *a priori*, theological conception of the 'sanctity' of the 'human' person. One has to admit that this is now more a privilege than a right, lacking as it does a right's capacity to be *really* general. Naturally so, because for this *a priori* presupposition it is not the real *historical* generality or universality characteristic of *mankind* which justifies that supposed right of private property, etc., but rather the unreal generality or universality of a *species transcending the human*. One can only confirm from this the present inadequacy of any justification made *a priori*, or on the basis of theology, especially in the broad sense of moral values. Human consciousness continues and will continue to ask for *rights*, but theology – even of the most thoroughly lay type – cannot *now* guarantee anything other than *privileges*. This is the *axiological powerlessness* – an inability to guarantee values – of all *a priorism* or *spiritualism*: a paradox, it may be admitted, but now obvious and irreversible.

2

Let us see how this *axiological powerlessness* now equally characterizes the morality of the discoverer of the moral imperative *par excellence* – the moral imperative as *categorical imperative*, absolute and unconditional, endowed by reasons which 'ordains by itself, *independently* of all the *facts*, that which *should* happen'.[1]

What at first glance could seem more *rational* and hence more *human* than the Kantian call to recognize that 'in the world, and even outside the world, there is nothing that can unconditionally be taken as good except *good will*'?[2] Nothing, that is, except for 'the will which is good for itself', inasmuch as it has the form of good will, will which is purely rational or universal, or 'will of the pure *form*'?[3]

Nothing, in short, can be taken as unconditionally good except the will directed 'towards universal ends', rather than one or other particular, accidental end or object in which there could be goodness, but a goodness only *apparent* because of its accidental, changeable nature. In any case, whatever the merits, certainly impressive, of this classic moral theory built up through the years, one must recognize that it too has had its day, precisely because the *rationality* round which it theorizes is too abstract and unreal to be human, and synonymous with *humanity*.

Let there be no doubt we do not mean, as it might appear and as basically many do think (just as still more, philosophers among them, think in a similar way of the 'essence', of the morality, of 'caritas'), that this is too 'high', too 'sublime' a morality for man to be capable or worthy of it. No, we mean simply that Kantian *moralism*, and modern moralism in general, is *today* obviously *inadequate* as a contribution to the formulation of those *human* values which, as specifically *moral* values, concern us above all others. This inadequacy forces us to reject moralism without indulging in dreams of a moral purism which, like almost all purisms, is at best a *rhetoric* that believes itself innocent.

First of all, let us look at the general presuppositions of the 'categorical imperative'.

According to Kant, man 'as a moral being', or 'person' is '*homo noumenon*' (reasoning man). He belongs, that is, to the suprasensible, the *intelligible* or *purely rational* world. *In that sense* he is a 'rational being' and 'true self' (*nur als Intelligenz das eigentliche Selbst*),[4] whilst man as a simple *animal rationale* is instead only *homo phaenomenon*, phenomenal man, or empirical, economic individual. Consequently *moral good* can only be constituted by the 'conception of the *law in itself*', exactly what occurs in a (pure) 'rational being', insofar as, in this being,' *only such a law* [or pure, intelligible universal] and *not an effect* hoped for as a result of action [or particular, phenomenon, for example] is the *determinant* of [moral] will'.[5] In other words, only insofar as will is determined by the '*immediate* conception of the law', by the pure universal, can moral good be constituted.

But [wonders Kant] what then can this law be, whose conception, *without concern for the effect*, must determine the will so that this may be termed *good absolutely* and unrestrictedly? Since I have eliminated from the will all the *impulses* which could be generated in it by results drawn from the observance of any [determinate] law, there is nothing left that can serve the will in principle except the *universal and generic conformity of actions to law*. In other words, I must always behave in such a way that I *can also will that the maxim I follow may become a universal law*. This is *simple generic conformity to law* (without taking as its foundation a law determinately governed by certain [particular] actions), which serves the will as its principle, and has in principle to serve it – *if duty is not an empty dream and a chimerical notion*.[6]

Thus are developed the synonymous concepts of '*disinterested interest*', 'intention', and 'good (or dutiful) will'. 'An *interest*,' says Kant 'is that for which *reason* becomes *practical*', or that for which it 'determines the will *immediately*',[7] as it is said. And 'the intention' is based on the purely intelligible in a '*suprasensible*' manner, given that '*virtue*' *par excellence* is that which, 'as a constant *intention* of fulfilling such actions *from duty*, for their morality ['duty for duty's sake', the universal because it is universal!], is called virtus noumenon,'[8] or '*noumenal*', or *intelligible*, virtue. How otherwise, Kant wonders, can the 'new "*Pauline*" man' have a *philosophical* sense – this man who 'in his new *intention* (*as intelligible being*) is morally an other in the eyes of a *divine judge* for whom *intention* takes the place of *action*.'[9] This is, let us note, Kantian 'interiority', and that of the *a priori* or theological *kind* in general. It is the *original inherence*, that is, *immediate*, not demonstrated, of the value or universal in the individual, which has as its consequence the radical devaluation of *exteriority*, *action*, of that *coming to grips* with the world in general which makes up the human being as worldly, *historical* being. Such is *traditional, abstract interiority* – the Platonic-Christian kind.

But, to continue, what if *reason* takes an *immediate* interest in action? 'Reason,' Kant replies, 'takes no immediate interest in action save when the *universal validity of the maxim* of such action is a *sufficient* principle of *determination* of the will.'[10] Only an *interest* of this kind is *pure*, and is a disinterested interest ('a taking of interest without, however, pursuing interest'). But when reason can only determine will through the means of an object of desire, or by inferring a particular sentiment in the subject, then it puts into operation only a *'mediated* interest'. This interest, which is *'empirical* and not at all a pure interest of reason', is not moral, and *has nothing to do with 'good' will*.[11] It can only be translated into a 'hypothetical imperative', which means that the action is good 'only conditionally', that is, 'in view of some [particular] end', but not yet as 'objectively necessary in itself, without reference to any [particular] end'.[12] Consequently, the simplest expression of the *'categorical* imperative', or 'absolute command' of the moral imperative is found in the famous phrase: 'Act *solely* according to the *maxim* which you can desire at the same time to become a *universal law*.'[13] For example, the maxim of action which prescribes the non-return of *money on deposit* entrusted to me, unless someone can show proof of the transaction, cannot be made a 'practical universal law', since such a principle of action 'as law' would destroy itself, in that 'it would mean *that there would be no more deposits*', that is, *no property*. One speaks in the same fashion of a 'false promise' and so forth.[14]

The weakness of this Kantian *moralism*, this ethical *purism*, does not actually lie where the post-Kantan ethical, romantic and self-styled historico-dialectical tradition, from Schiller to Croce, has seen it. Nor, if we dwell awhile on a more contemporary objection, does it lie in a moral *rigour*, an abstractness, which would *sacrifice* the individual, or passion, or the hedonistic 'concrete'. In this, in fact, is found moralism's historical merit as a corrective of hedonism and the Enlightenment's practical empiricism. It sees itself as corrective of the enlightenment *from within*, and its moralism coherently opens up the enlightenment principle of 'aude sapere', or 'have the courage to make use of your intellect', to its foundations.

Rather, its true weakness lies in a different *abstractness*, one shared by the romantics and idealists themselves, that is, by its very own traditional critics. This is the abstractness of the *original interiority* of value, of the *original*, metahistorical *person*. It is the abstractness of one who understands the constitution of the *person* by means of an extra-historical conferral of value, and who proposes to separate the human person and his dignity and related rights from the value or universal which only the *person* can really confer. That is, the person is separated from the historical value, or universal, present in the human species or universal, and specifically in the non-metaphorical, non-mystical community or *society* of human interests. Hence, in the last resort, the extra-historical, original person can only be a *privileged* individual because he is *abnormal*, or abstract, free from what is normal for his species. His original, extra-historical ('eternal'), 'natural' *rights*, are nothing but justifications of real, actual *privileges*.

Therefore, *rather than sacrificing the individual, Kantian moralism* (and idealist moralism in general) *exalts and frustrates him*. Let us examine this carefully. It so happens that if man is moral only as 'noumenal', or purely rational man, thereby excluding phenomenal man or the empirical, self-interested, economic individual, then he cannot count on *empirical* suggestions. He cannot count on them in his action by reason of making the assumption of 'duty for its own sake', or *the universal for the sake of the universal*, which is the practical assumption of a purely rational being, such as he wishes to be. Empirical suggestions arise from practical experience of the merely human, historical world, which surrounds him with particular, circumstantial problems of *living in society*.

He is instead forced to act according to a norm of absolute idealization, dogmatic in its own intentions, which can in fact have as its own irreducible content only the phenomenal, empirical, economic individual in his *immediacy*. A norm without content, or one which can express nothing, is nonsense. Thus, that phenomenal, particular man persists not only because of the irreducible requirement that there must be a content for the form or norm, but persists as a content or particular *not mediated* by the form or universal, not really infused or modified by the norm. He persists, that is, exactly to the extent that he must be sacrificed to 'noumenal', rational-pure man, to achieve moral man. The norm itself, as one of absolute idealization or universalization, dogmatic, and *not* critically verified against the *human* world which is *social* because it is historical, *has transcended this very world*. And that content or particular remains as immediate content, as phenomenal or economic man, but seen as *abstract*, *abnormal*, and *asocial*.

In other words, one could say that the purity of the *a priori*, nontemporal universal, of the purely formal 'moral law', in fact shows its powerlessness to overcome the *gratuitousness* of the temporal-particular, or content. This gratuitousness is *caused precisely by the act of transcending content*. However, the genuine requirement for the *universal* as *functional criterion*, or as *unifying* a diversity, is also debased. This *genuine unitary* demand is debased in its *false version*, which is that of its *purity*, by the *continuous oscillation* between the inhuman purity of the non-temporal universal and the blind wilfulness (both too little human and too much!) of the *non-integrated*, non-mediated (because transcended) temporal-particular – and back again. In this way Kant's famous 'utilitarianism' could be explained – that unexpected, 'surreptitious' *utilitarianism*, in which *rigourism* is turned upside down. It would be explained as a *theological utilitarianism*, a utilitarianism arising from a transcendental, *a priori*, abstract basis of moral value.

Think, in fact, of the utilitarian, economic estimation of the 'consequences' of violating that moral law which is so strict, in the example of the sum of money entrusted to me, whereby there would be no more money deposited in the world, and no more security of property. But think not only of the abstractness, falseness, and immorality of the Kantian requirement in itself, which means that if the owner of the deposit were insane, or an enemy of the community, it would be obligatory, as was observed earlier, not to return the money, and so forth. Rather, think of the motive, which is not a chance one, and of the intrinsic reason, behind this abstractness and immorality. Consider the very Kantian concept of the moral law, in which the absoluteness of the law creates by means of its own abstractness, of its own 'immediateness', the abstractness and rigidity of its content or particular. Its content, inasmuch as it is transcended by the law, is precisely not integrated or modified by the law but remains *for this reason surreptitiously*, secretly, corruptly present. In this instance, it is present as a blind *asocial* instinct of property.

Likewise, we can discuss the case of the 'false promise': how many times can a false promise be a strict obligation? – and of the case of the 'lie' in general, with respect to which Kant very candidly states that this 'need *not* be harmful to *others* for it to be condemned'[15] and so forth. Thus one understands, and explains, even if one no longer excuses, the internal coherence of Kant's rigorous *natural law theory*. This lies in the principle of 'entering society (*if you cannot avoid it*) with others, so that in it each may *preserve* what belongs to him'.[16] Here are 'rights' as 'natural rights', *a priori*, or particular *privileges* of the original, presocial, pre-historical person. Thus is explained the purely negative, formal concept of *right*, in which 'every right consists *solely* in the *limitation* of the freedom of each'.[17]

This is indeed the concept, as the Kantian Martinetti puts it, of a 'realm of external liberty *in the light of the realm of internal liberty*', in the light, as we know, of the abstract liberty which is the original liberty of the person endowed with an original, *a priori* 'interiority' of values. Hereby is explained the basic premise – 'innate *equality* is the same as *independence*'[18] – in which connection it must be admitted that it is a very clever definition of equality which at once turns it into its antithesis, into liberty! In addition, it can be explained that the ideal society is a 'kingdom of *ends in themselves*'[19] which are the 'rational beings', understood in Kant's terms as purely rational and hence moral entities, as it were an *aggregate of monads*, certainly not a *society* or *community worthy of the name*. It is almost superfluous to add that this *ethical narcissism*, insofar as it is *spiritual narcissism*, narcissism of abstract *interiority*, radically devalues *labour*, that typical mediation of interior and exterior, which inserts us into the human world, that of living in society. It devalues labour and prefers virtues whose value lies not in 'results', not in the 'uses' they produce, but in 'intentions'. 'Skill', he says 'and diligence in *labour* have a *market price* [*Marktpreis*] [. . .]; on the other hand *fidelity to promises*, *benevolence in principle* (not instinctive benevolence) have an *intrinsic value* [*innern Wert*].'[20]

Here we can see in what, specifically and finally, the Kantian *Würde des Menschen*, the 'dignity of man', consists.[21] It is only the '*dignity* of *man-as-bourgeois*', in that the obligation to 'humanity in the person', whose being is the practical, obligatory recognition of this dignity, is only obligation to the *intelligible* or rational-pure being – ourselves and others. That is, it is only the obligation of 'truthfulness', 'respect' and 'love' towards *humanity in an ahistorical, asocial person*. Hence it is *inhuman*, and this conception of dignity in fact is the *dignity of pure interiority*, abstracted from the exteriority and worldliness which is that of social coexistence, or the *typical* social character of *labour*. From this, the morality of *duty for duty's sake*, or the *universal for the sake of the universal*, *moralism*, is the morality not of human, social, complete man, but of that partial man – the *individualist* man, class-man, precisely *common-bourgeois* man. *Surreptitious utilitarianism* insofar as it is *theological*, and ethical *narcissism* insofar as it is *spiritual*, mark his unsurpassable limits, and the fate of his *class* morality, in which 'Christian individualism', traditional abstract individualism, reaches its highest point (see below, *Clarifications*, 3).

3

As for Rousseau's specifically political philosophy, one should start by recalling the conclusion of the *Discourse on the origin and foundations of inequality among men*, on which the tone of the formulation of the 'fundamental problem', which the *Social Contract* is to resolve, depends.

The conclusion says that *'moral* [or "civil"] *inequality*, legitimated by positive law alone, is *contrary* to *natural right* each time it does *not* coincide in the *same proportion* with *physical inequality'* [or immediate individual inequality of 'strength' and 'talent', etc.][1] It poses, therefore, the demand of conformity to pure *reason* (to *'natural* right') of moral, i.e. civil or social, inequality, as proportional to the immediate or empirical inequality of strength, talent, etc., between one individual and another. That is, the rational conformity of an *equality*, or justice, consisting of a proportionality of inequalities both individual-empirical and of value, is understood as conformity to *natural right*. It is understood as the *rationality* of equality harmonized from those so-called proportional inequalities, in which each of the *natural liberties* consists – those liberties of man *'independent* by *nature'*, or according to his *pure*, rational *essence* – man, to put it clearly, as *a priori person*, meta-historical, pre-social. This is the demand in which *equality* is indeed understood as a *function of liberty*, or ultimately of the person, but *not also vice versa*. The person, indeed, to whom all natural liberty is here attributed, is the independent, abstract, asocial man, the man *essentially alien* to the manner of existing which is coexistence, or living in society, or *sociality*, in which the demand for *equality* or *justice* has a *positive* and *specific meaning*. 'Innate *equality is the same as independence.*' So Kant, the master of natural law theory, logically defines equality, thereby at the outset dogmatically reducing equality to its contrary, liberty, by a striking simplification of the moral problematic, and one which ends by threatening liberty itself.

But let us move on to the formulation of the *fundamental*

problem the *Social Contract* has to solve. It expresses the need to 'find a form of *association* which can *defend* and *protect* with all its common strength the *person* and *goods* of each member [that is, sanctions those *demands of value*, viewed as *rational pure* individual *rights* which, like the *person and the goods* are corollaries of the natural law or *a priori* proportional moral and individual empirical inequalities], and by means of which each, uniting himself with all, still obeys only himself and stays as *free as before*'.[2] That is, he must find an association in which he may remain independent man according to nature. From this it seems clear that contractual-political formalism, which should mediate 'nature' or *reason* and *history*, and thus make the *common man*, the human *person*, real, turns out now to be an overly extrinsic means to be able to justify anything other than a mere *political liberty* as historical *copy* or *a posteriori* translation of *natural* or *a priori liberties*. This appears, in fact, as an 'artificial', unnatural means, in the sense in which states are termed 'large artificial bodies'.

There is a final consequence of the suggestion of an 'equality' of the kind instituted by the clause in the social contract. In this, the 'social pact' sets up a 'moral and *legitimate equality*' of such a kind among men that they, 'though being unequal in strength and talent, *all* become *equal* by *convention* and of right.'[3] It is an equality, in short, which is *moral* and *legitimate* insofar as it is *conventional-artificial*, or positive (public) law. I.e. that *formal* equality, or equality *before the law* is none other than *formal* or political liberty, the copy of the *natural* liberties which indicate equality as function of liberty, but not also vice versa! Indeed, Marx saw astutely that 'it was a question of the *liberty* of *man* as an isolated *monad*'[4] when in *On the Jewish Question* – itself inspired by the best of Rousseau in its profound egalitarianism, as we shall see – he commented on article 6 on *liberty* defined as '*the power which man possesses to do everything which does not harm the rights of others*'.[5] This is the 'most radical' and Rousseauan article of the French constitution of 1793.

There, Marx concludes that 'the droits de l'homme *as distinct from* the droits de citoyen', 'natural' rights in fact, 'are nothing but the rights of a member of *civil* society', man 'enclosed in his particular interest and his particular opinion, *separated* from the *community*'.[6] That equality or *justice is liberty*, and that in short the thesis immediately becomes its own antithesis, is the *contradictio in adiecto* (logical contradiction) the basic deficiency, in which (in the eyes of modern criticism) Rousseau seems trapped. One recalls, for example, Kelsen's* remark, one-sided though it is, on the 'original anarchic tendency' of Rousseauan democratic 'liberty'.

In other words, the *simplemindedness*, and the subsequent sterility, of the *a priori* Rousseauan *solution* of the main problem of equality as *proportionality* of *inequalities* of value, or individual empirical inequalities, is now revealed. This solution rests on the conception of *this equality-proportionality* as a *natural right*, or the pre-social natural liberties of the individual. An equality so conceived is as far from being able to justify a legitimate equality *for all* as *political-natural* liberty (to which it is reduced) as it is far from being real liberty or liberty *for all*. Political-natural liberty is abstract, pre-social liberty, a 'free enterprise', *fortuitous*, *bourgeois*, partial, bourgeois-*class* liberty – or substantial unfreedom. This means ultimately admitting the *lack of mediation* between value and the empirical, or the failure fully to explain the composition of the empirical, concrete individual as individual-value which results from the aforesaid *proportionality* of *inequalities*, *if taken in the light of natural law theory*, and in an *a priori* manner (see 5 and II, 7 and *Clarifications*, 4).

This is the – unconscious – theory of the disequilibrium of liberty and justice which invalidates the premises of the Rousseauan 'social compact', one of the models of 'bourgeois democracy'. This is the ideology which Kant

* Hans Kelsen (1881–1973). German-American legal philosopher, influenced by neo-Kantianism. Cf. his *General Theory of Law and the State* (English-language translation, 1943).

too makes his own, making it more understandable and undoubtedly making it worse. Thus Kant, having postulated that '*innate* equality is the same as independence' can logically conclude: 'one enters society (if you cannot avoid it) with others, so that in it each may *preserve* what belongs to him.' He makes a corollary of the purely formal, negative, related concept of *law*, by which 'every law consists *solely* in the *delimitation* of the liberty of each.' Hence we find the *Kantian* conclusion, which contains a *perfect* summary of the parable of the man independent 'by nature', or the *a priori* person, who is constituted as a *privileged person* by means of the *a priori* (innate independence-equality!) and his consequent pre-sociality ('enter, if you cannot avoid, society', etc.).

The aim is that *each* may *preserve* in society what *already* belongs to him! Here it is clear that if *society* is a *posterius*, and something inessential, not 'all', not everyone, but *only some* can *preserve in it* (as an 'apparent' society) that which *natural independence* (the *prius*) with its *individual differences made absolute* has in fact obtained for them. Yet, to qualify this, it has been correctly observed by Solari[7] that 'while for Rousseau the contract means renouncing the state and liberty of nature and the creation of a new moral and social order, for Kant it introduces no novelty to the natural juridical order and simply tends to consolidate and make it real in a more perfect and rational form' (see further on, the end of the first part of this work, for *this* Rousseau).

In Rousseau, one must compare the *legitimation* of that *metaphysical hendiadys* whose terms are *persons and goods* (a true and exact hypostasis). And, to go no further, one must consider the characteristic *absoluteness*, or abstractness and *inhumanity*, which traditional, bourgeois law lends to 'possessions' and which is precisely, theoretically, formulated as an *attribute* of the person-substance – the man-of-nature or *man-a priori* (with his corresponding 'holiness'). This *right* is now revealed as a *privilege*, insofar as it is the negation of the demand of value or *universality*, or demand concerning *each*, which constitutes justice, the potential essence of right. The *privileged person*, therefore, indicates to the contemporary critic the most typical and concentrated contradiction in the terms of ethico-juridical, bourgeois, class ideology – that is, the person, or individual-value, who is privileged – in other words, the negation of value!

Therefore, the futility of Rousseau's *contractualism* as justification of a mediation of reason and history or experience is confirmed in the particular, insofar as it derives from the concept of rationality as *pure reason* or reason *a priori*, innate ('nature'!), and cannot grasp the historical act, or social act, except as a simple expedient or 'artificial' instrument of reason and society – in short, as an absolute *posterius*. However, as a consequence, the need to abandon the criterion of a *pure* or *meta-historical* rationality in favour of that of a *material* or *historical rationality* is revealed. This permits the identification of the middle term between reason and experience in *society* as *social* value. The bankruptcy of this term in natural law theory and contract theory has led them into the contradictions and deficiencies demonstrated above.

In short, one cannot deny (who would?) the revolutionary function fulfilled for centuries by 'natural law' in general, as regards the contribution on the ideological level to changing a social reality characterized above all by political subjection. This begins (to go no further back) with Pufendorf and his *Christian individualism*, in which everyone draws the right to liberty from the power of whoever is his *equal in God*, and finishes with Locke, Rousseau, and Kant, who posit the final demand of realizing *humanitarian*, or lay-Christian equality, of 'natural' right, on the basis of 'civil right', or political right. This last replaces the 'royal edicts' with 'the law' as 'expression of popular will', derived from the 'contract'. In this, the secular function of the Platonic-Christian, or *a priori* religious, metaphysical, conception of 'human nature' as 'likeness of God', etc., reaches its highest point, in a conception to which is owed the first discovery of the *human universal*, of that *common man* unknown to the city of antiquity. If, then, the above is undeniable, one must on the other hand admit that once the natural law, metaphysical, ideological cycle – that of abstract rationalism – had been historically exhausted by its now recognized inability to mediate further between reason and history as a result of its *hypostases*, and hence its inability to grasp history, the revolutionary function of ideology could only belong thereafter to a concrete or materialist rationalism. This rationalism is one which could fully work out an historical-experimental, *sociological* conception of man and the person.

4

Another prime example of Christianity's 'cult of abstract man' is the Lockean natural-law justification of *labour*, the cause of so much equivocation in so-called social-reformist criticism, and for which it is worth opening a parenthesis. It is, in fact, the conception of Locke the *deist* or, if one prefers, the 'reasonable' theist, that *labour* itself is the *property* of the human *person* as *subject* of *natural* or innate, or *rational pure, rights*, preceding the (historical) incorporation of man into society. He says: 'All that man undertakes as *labouring activity* to procure comfort and sustenance for his own existence [. . .] *belongs entirely to him* and is *not* already property *common to all*.' So 'labour', like 'life', 'personal liberty' and 'possessions', is the 'property' – and 'right' – of 'men free and independent by nature', who are joined together in 'political communities' only by subsequent 'contract', which has the aim of 'preserving' '*these rights*' reciprocally. At once it becomes clear that precisely in the Lockean-natural-law concept of *labour power* or 'labouring activity' as *property-right* of the human *person*, lies the *philosophical* or most general, foundation of the *bourgeois* economic conception of labour power as something *private*, and hence a fortuitous occasion for relations between individual and individual. In short, it is an object of *exchange*, a *commodity* (and not only the founda-

tion of *private* property in *cultivated* land, as Locke argues.)
'This sphere that we are deserting, within whose boundaries the sale and purchase of labour-power goes on, is
in fact a very *Eden of the innate rights of man*' (cited above as
epigraph).[1]

Thus, even from a rapid examination of this typical
aspect of Lockean natural law theory, there is proof for us
of the present unfoundedness of the conception of the
person as subject of pure natural or rational rights.
Consider, in particular, the open contradition between
labour, or the specific action of the *person* or individual-
value that is *man*, and its being understood as *commodity*, a
thing and, in short, as something *inhuman* – an antinomy
demonstrated by the passage from Marx quoted above as
epigraph. Here one sees only how contradictory and vain
is the social-reformist or social-liberal claim to make the
socialist demand, even in practice, a kind of mere *appendix* of
the natural-law-theory *Declaration of the rights of man and
citizen*. As Marx said, already giving a fitting critical
definition of natural rights, these are 'droits de l'homme as
distinct from the droits du citoyen.'[2] For it is evident that if
one starts from the Lockean concept of labour as
'original', a natural right of the person, as in Rodolfo
Mondolfo, for example, and hence from the concept of
surplus labour and surplus value as an 'offence against a
natural right', one will only arrive at claims merely
concerning the *extent* of capitalist exploitation of labour,
or the *containing* of such exploitation – as in the reformist
'legal barriers' concerning hours of labour, the level of
wages, and other *humanitarian* objectives. But one will
never arrive at claims regarding exploitation itself and its
abolition. The *natural* right of the owner of capital, of the
buyer of labour power, will in fact always counterbalance
the natural right of the owner of labour power, its seller.

In other words, how can surplus value and profit be
logically described as an 'injustice of *division*' of the
products, from the point of view of natural right, as
Mondolfo and so many others argue, if productive labour

power is *private* according to natural law theory, which means it is the property-right of the person-worker and hence can be alienated at will with its products? A '*social division*' of the product, from this point of view, is truly a 'nonsense' as too is Marxist surplus value. But this is not because both are only 'in economics' as Benedetto Croce thinks, but on the contrary insofar as they are *already* within natural right or the metaphysical (theological) cult of abstract man or of the 'philosophy of the *spirit*', as in the case of Croce. For a properly severe, but naïve, and non-motivated, critique of Lockean natural law theory see Heinrich Rommen, *Die ewige Wiederkehr des Naturrechts* (*The eternal return of natural law*) (Munich: Kösel, 1947, p. 91). This adversely criticizes the characteristic of 'individualism', and hence the predominance of '*iustitia commutativa*' (commutative justice) or *exchange*, and of the egoistic interest raised above, and against, the '*iustitia distributiva et legalis*' (distributive, legal justice) and the common good. This is a naïve and inconclusive critique since it is inspired not only by a modern natural law theorist in the name of the metaphysical and moral order of being, against the empirical Lockean 'catalogue' of individual, egotistical rights,[3] but in addition, because it is by a catholic, by a neo-Thomist.

5

But, returning to Rousseau, there is still much to look at. One must examine the *positive* legacy he leaves us and see exactly how much of his original philosophico-political *problematic* is not historically exhausted (in the course of the bourgeois revolution), and becomes a fruitful ferment on a later historical plane, and hence a guiding element, resolvable in, and by means of, a different philosophico-political method. The method of an original spiritualist-humanitarian, and, in short, *a priori*, *solution* has now collapsed, since it is historically exhausted and not revivable, as shown in our critique above. In particular, one is concerned to see what may remain of the peculiarly

Rousseauan problems in the *development*, still in progress, of modern *democracy* – which are also in the problematic of scientific socialism. And by this is meant *something very different* from the traditional, social-liberal reduction, both *external* and *mechanical*, of the *socialist* demand to a mere formal *appendix* to the *Declaration of the Rights of man and citizen*, with its relative, partial, exhausted, Rousseauan content. Indeed, we have called this an external and mechanical reduction, since it is a reduction, let us be clear, *not* permitted at all by what the *democratic* demand preserves, and which is specific and historically not exhausted. This demand figures in Rousseau, and not in Locke or Kant or Humboldt; not, that is, in the theorists of the specifically *liberal* demand, and hence that of the *Rechtstaat*, the quintessence of the bourgeois, parliamentary-constitutional state.

To concern ourselves briefly with Kant, and his pupil Wilhelm von Humboldt* (we shall deal later with the political philosophy of Locke and his heirs), it is enough to recall the presupposition underlying their *Rechtstaat* or *State of law* as that type of state whose *sole* aim is to guarantee the the 'juridical order' and, in particular, the rights of personal liberty and property of the citizens – 'security' as Humboldt put it.[1] This presupposes in both men a substantial lack of interest in the democratic-egalitarian, typically Rousseauan, demand; and interest instead, and only, in the liberal-democratic, or libertarian, or specifically bourgeois demand. Already, at a glance, the negative Kantian conception, indicated above, of human labour as an activity which has only a market price and no dignity, is anti-egalitarian (on its juridical consequences in the liberal-Kantian system, see *Clarifications*, 3).

With this we come to the decisive point: what can still remain of the Rousseauan problematic that was not exhausted in the *Declaration* of 1789? How, in short, does

* Wilhelm von Humboldt (1767–1835), political philosopher and linguist. Combined an idealist view of history with individualistic humanism.

Rousseau transcend the bourgeois revolution historically, that revolution which, as Marx thought, had its most adequate and basic reflection in Kantian *Rechtslehre* (legal doctrine)? What does it still contribute to the further – and present – development of modern democracy? We have already met up with this problematic *issue* and have only subjected the natural-law, *a priori*, solution to criticism – its formula revealed now as abstract, and hence unsuitable for prolonging the historical fertility of the problematic. The live issue, which is the very substance of the Rousseauan original problematic, is the conception of the *rationality of an equality which consists in a universal proportionality based on inequalities or differences of (civil or social) value, and individual-empirical differences*. It is the conception of an *egalitarian, but not levelling, society*.

It is a society so constructed as to realize in and for itself a type of equality or justice consisting of a universal proportionality of social differences, and of personal differences of worth (strength, talent, etc.). This proportionality is universal inasmuch as it is ensured by the 'common strength' of the 'social body' or true 'sovereign' – the society in and for itself which realizes . . . and so on, exactly as has been stated. However, the original contractualist, natural-law summation of this kind of society permitted, as we have seen, the guarantee of the merits and hence the rights of only *a part* of the *individuals* constituting the social body, only one class, the bourgeoisie ('to find a form of association which can defend and protect with all its common strength the *person and goods* of each member.')[2] In this society, the key concepts of 'general' will of the social body, and 'popular' sovereignty were in fact found to be contradicted. However, it is also true that the original democratic problematic of Rousseau, with its own radical conception of a *unitary* sovereign body and of the latter's decisive rational-artificial-historical character, already threatens to destroy the rational – natural – *a priori* formulation of natural-law theory which, we know, is not that of Kant!

Thus, the problem uncovered by Rousseau, of the *social* recognition of the *individual* himself, or of the universal proportionality in social values and individual merits described above – the problem, in short, of *egalitarian liberty* – remains a real *problem* even after the bourgeois revolution, and still awaits its complete solution. We must see how, in the complex context of the historical-ideal development of modern democracy, this problem can be completely solvable by virtue of a method very different from that of Rousseau's rationalist-voluntarist-abstract, or spiritualist-humanitarian, method.[3] This alternative method, expressed above as that of a concrete or materialist rationalism, is that of scientific socialism, Marxist–Leninist sociological method, which replaces the useless principle of interclassism as justified by traditional, Rousseauan humanitarianism. By this method too it replaces all utopian 'socialism' and all revisionist 'Marxism' or social-liberalism, with the principle of class, class struggle.

NOTES

Section 1

1. Marx, *Capital*, vol. 1 (Moore–Aveling translation) (Moscow: Progress, 1965), p. 79.
2. ibid., p. 176 (della Volpe's emphases).
3. J.-J. Rousseau, *Emile, ou l'éducation*, Bk iv (*Œuvres complètes*, 4 (Paris: Gallimard, 1969)), pp. 493, 523.
4. ibid., pp. 600–1.
5. ibid., p. 632.
6. ibid., note to p. 523.
7. ibid., p. 614.
8. *The Journals of Søren Kierkegaard* (ed. Alexander Dru) (Oxford: OUP, 1938), p. 370.
9. Emile, op. cit., pp. 595–6.
10. Rousseau, *Julie ou La Nouvelle Héloïse*, pt 5, letter 8 (*Œuvres complètes*, 2 (Paris: Gallimard, 1961)), p. 612.
11. Rousseau, *Du contrat social*. Ch. 6, Bk 1 (*Œuvres complètes*, 3 (Paris: Gallimard, 1962)), p. 360.
12. ibid.
13. ibid., p. 362.

Section 2

1. Kant, *Fundamental Principles of the Metaphysic of Morals* (1785), (*Grundlegung zur Metaphysik der Sitten*), 2nd section.
2. ibid., 1st section.
3. ibid., 3rd section.
4. ibid.
5. ibid., 1st section.
6. ibid., 2nd section.
7. ibid., 3rd section.
8. Kant, *Religion within the bounds of pure reason* (1793) (*Religion innerhalb der Grenzen der blossen Vernunft*), Preface to the second edition.
9. ibid., second part, 1st section.
10. *Fundamental Principles*, op. cit., 3rd section.
11. ibid.
12. ibid., 2nd section.
13. ibid.
14. Kant, *Critique of Practical Reason* (1788), (*Kritik der praktischen Vernunft*), Bk 1, pt 1.
15. Kant, *Metaphysics of Morals* (1797), (*Die Metaphysik der Sitten*) *The Metaphysical Elements of the Theory of Virtue*, Bk 1, pt 1.
16. ibid., Introduction, Theory of right.
17. 'On the commonplace which is good in theory but worthless in practice' (1793 article).
18. Introduction, op. cit.
19. *Fundamental Principles*, op. cit., 2nd section.
20. ibid.
21. ibid.

Section 3

1. Rousseau, *Discours sur l'origine et les fondements de l'inégalité* (*Œuvres complètes*, 3 (Paris: Gallimard, 1962), Conclusion, pp. 193–4.
2. *Du contrat social*, Ch. 6, Bk 1, op. cit., p. 360
3. ibid., Ch. 9, Bk 1, p. 367
4. Marx, *On the Jewish Question* (Collected Works, vol. 3 (London: Lawrence and Wishart, 1975), p. 162).
5. Quoted in ibid., p. 162.
6. Della Volpe translates this as *bourgeois* society: the last quotation is retranslated.
7. See section 5, note 1.

Section 4

1. See note 2, section 1.
2. See note 6, section 3.
3. e.g. Locke '[. . .] *maximum* enim *munimentum rei cujusque privatae lex*

est naturae, sine cujus observatione rem suam possidere suisque commodis inservire nemini licet', etc. ('for the *strongest protection of each man's private property* is the *law* of nature, without the observance of which it is impossible for anybody to be master of his property and to pursue his own advantage' (John Locke, *Essays on the Law of Nature*, ed. W. von Leyden (Oxford: OUP, 1954), pp. 206–7).

Section 5

1. In the letter to Forster, 1 June 1792, (*Briefe*, Munich: Hanser, 1952, p. 70): 'The *preservation of security* [. . .] (is) uniquely a state institution. If the activity of the state were greatly increased, private initiative would be limited in a prejudicial manner, only uniformity would be produced and, in a word, the internal formation of man would be damaged.' See too the essay on the limits of state activity: *Thoughts on an attempted definition of state action* (Munich, 1954). (*Ideem zu einem Versuch, die Grenzen der Wirksamkeit des Staats zu bestimmen*).

Note especially parts III, IV and V, on the two basic theses – 1, that the 'concern of the State for the *positive well-being* of the citizens prevents the development of human individuality and personality': 2, that, on the other hand, 'the concern of the State for the *negative well-being* of the citizens, for their security', should simply 'constitute the aim of the State'.

For Kant, see the *Metaphysics of Morals*, 1. The *Metaphysical Elements of the Theory of Right*, 1797, Italian translation by G. Solari and G. Vidari in *Kant, Scritti politici e di filosofia della storia e del diritto*, ed. N. Bobbio, L. Firpo, V. Mathieu, (Turin: Utet, 1956) pp. 377–567: and see further on, *Clarifications*, 3. In that volume see, for instance, the following highly interesting *historical* observation by the late Gioele Solari in his fine *Introduction* (pp. 11–46): 'Kant shows himself particularly severe on ethical despotism, both in the personal, empirical, enlightened form of his own country [the paternalist State, against which Humboldt's first thesis already rebelled, as above], and in the rational, democratic form of Rousseau. The State which wishes to realize individual happiness or collective morality by coercive means, does not achieve its goal and becomes oppressive [. . .] The personality of man in his natural and moral needs has also for Kant an absolute value, and can neither exist nor develop without the free, direct action of the individual. In this almost religious cult of the personality, Kant can call himself deeply *liberal* and consequently *anti-democratic* [. . .] Kant did *not* accept the *egalitarian* need implicit in *democratic* doctrine', etc. (emphasis by GdV). Note too the following: 'The former [Locke's 'empirical liberalism'] was only ever a *class* liberalism with an economic content, the other [Rousseau's 'ethical liberalism'] a State liberalism, governed by non-juridical ends. The liberal idea found in Kant a *universal* juridical form [. . .] Kant's criticism [. . .] developed with particular harshness [. . .] against enlightened despotism. [. . .] the paternal State, guardian of the individual. [. . .] *Neither* can the Kantian juridical State be confused with Rousseau's ethico-political universalism, which sacrifices the *natural* right and liberty of the individual [but see further on 11, 6–7, and *Classifications*, 4] to establish through the state *a new order of reason*, from which the individual derives his right and in which all particularisms are resolved', etc. (GdV's emphasis).

All these are observations which the Kantian Solari expressed with particular clarity – even at the risk of error: that whole contradictory, partly muddled, liberal-democratic problematic of modern democracy, on which see above and further on (Solari, as a Kantian, is superior not only to the modern followers of neo-Thomist natural-law theory, like Rommen whom we quoted, but also to the Hegelian state-worshippers). For our purpose, it is sufficient here to note: 1, that there is no rigorous significance, either historical or philosophical, in taking Lockean liberalism as a class phenomenon and then denying the same characteristic in Kantian liberalism. 'Through Kant's theory', argues Solari, 'the liberal State ceases to be the State of a particular epoch or class, and is shown to be the State in which man, in the wholeness of his empirical and rational nature, is eternally satisfied'. For, as seen earlier, it is precisely by Kant's *generalities* and *hypostases*, that is, by his systematic and logical natural-law theory, that the internal logic of the abstract or 'sacred' man in the bourgeois person is made manifest – the internal logic of *dogmatic individualism* (but on the complexity of the assessment of Kant, see II, 7 and *Clarifications*, 3). The same holds for Rousseau, we know, although with necessary major reservations about his original egalitarian problematic, which thus already breaks with the natural-law plan (see here, further on and 11, 6–7, and *Clarifications*, 3). 2, that the great confusion about, and widespread condemnation of, the (democratic) centralism of sovereign popular power, with its relative 'ethico-political universalism', and of more or less enlightened despotism, reflects the limits of the juridical-*formal*-bourgeois, abstract, point of view. This is the product of natural-law theory, and, definitely, of class interests, of which it is the philosophical expression. It is hence destined to disappear with them. However, it is also destined to remain widespread in the most diverse forms, as it still remains today in the general political attribute of 'totalitarianism', so long as the natural law *dogma* of the Rechtstaat and its underlying interests persists (for the full answer to the charge of 'totalitarianism' made against democratic-socialist centralism, see II, 6–7, and the last note, on the analysis of the concept of 'socialist legality').

2. *Du contrat social*, op. cit., p. 360.

3. Bourgeois revolutionary technique, whose principle is the 'political intellect' or rationalist abstract voluntarism, or that of enlightenment *raison*, with its powerlessness in the face of the natural limits presented by the economic reality it fails to observe, and with its implicit inability to discover the reasons for 'social deficiencies', are brilliantly synthesized by the young Marx in this profile of Robespierre's Rousseauan mentality: 'The *classic* period of political intellect is the *French revolution*. Far from seeing the source of social shortcomings in the [economic] principle of the state, the heroes of the French revolution instead saw in social defects the source of political evils. Thus *Robespierre* saw in great poverty and great wealth only an obstacle to *pure democracy*. Therefore he wished to establish a *Spartan* frugality. The principle of politics is the *will*. The more one-sided [abstract] the political intellect, and therefore the more perfected, the more does it believe in the *omnipotence* of the will, [the more it is blind to the *natural* and spiritual *limits* of the will,] and the more incapable it is, therefore, of discovering the [economic] source of social ills' ('Critical Marginal notes on the article "The King of Prussia and social reform. By a Prussian" ' (*Vorwärts*, Paris, 7 August 1844, no. 63); *Collected Works*, vol. 3 (London: Lawrence and Wishart, 1975), p. 199.

II

THE PROBLEM OF EGALITARIAN LIBERTY IN THE DEVELOPMENT OF MODERN DEMOCRACY; OR, THE LIVING ROUSSEAU

I thought that to be provided with talents was the surest provision against poverty.

Rousseau[1]

Every right is an application of an equal measure to different men [. . .] That is why 'equal right' is a violation of equality and an injustice.

Marx[2]

. . . an existence guaranteeing to all the free development and exercise of their physical and mental faculties.

Engels[3]

6

The conclusions of Norberto Bobbio's essay on 'Democracy and dictatorship' (in *Politica e cultura* (Turin: Einaudi, 1955), pp. 148 ff. and cf. pp. 150 ff.) invite one to investigate the basic problems of modern political philosophy, and can provide a point of departure for further surprising conclusions, different, at least in part, from those of the author. He invites us, basically, to apply ourselves to the hardest and most mysterious problematic puzzle of the modern theory of democracy: the complex and ambiguous relationship between liberalism (Locke, Kant, Humboldt, Constant, etc.,) and democracy (Rousseau, Marx, Engels).

The contrast [he says,] between the Soviet regime and Western regimes is not a contrast between democracy and nondemocracy, or between greater and lesser democracy, but between dictatorial regime and liberal regime. It is not, in short, the greater degree of democracy (either in the sense of government by the people or government for the people) that the liberal boasts of over the communist, but of the greater freedom which, for the liberal, is the presupposition (right or wrong, but this has to be demonstrated) of the very functioning of democracy. It is worth emphasising the fact that Lenin's polemical phrase 'Proletarian democracy is a thousand times more *democratic* than any bourgeois democracy', which may sound excessive but is not contradictory, would sound incorrect if we changed it to 'Proletarian democracy is a thousand times more *liberal* than any bourgeois democracy.'[4]

In general this is correct, and Kelsen had, we shall see, already shown the extraordinarily democratic character of the Soviet regime. However, what a hornet's nest of 'showing' and defining this aroused! Meanwhile, the first impression is that one is again hearing an old tune, essentially the charge brought by the 'impenitent liberal' Benjamin Constant – as Halbwachs called him for this specific remark – against Rousseau and his *democratic* conception of sovereignty: 'It is untrue,' said Constant, 'that the whole society possesses unlimited sovereignty over its members [. . .]. Rousseau's error made the social contract, so often invoked in favour of liberty, the most frightening aid of every type of despotism' (Halbwachs's edition of Rousseau's *Contrat social*, p. 112; Paris: Aubier-Montaigne, 1967).

But let us look a little closer. It is true that in the previous pages Bobbio tries to show the legitimacy of 'the need to ask the defenders of the dictatorship of the proletariat to consider the form of *liberal*-democratic regime for the value of its more refined and progressive juridical technique' (my emphasis). And he tries to propose again to these 'defenders' the principle of the 'separation of powers' (Locke-Montesquieu).

So [he says] official thinking in the USSR energetically rejects this principle, arguing that 'the Soviet social order is infused by the general spirit of the uniqueness of the authority of the workers', as if there were a conflict between the uniqueness of the source of sovereignty and division of the organs which exercise it, and as though the very principle of the source of power, so-called national or popular sovereignty, was not already a traditionally bourgeois doctrine. Clearly there is a confusion here between the basis of authority, which rests on civil society, and the means by which this authority is exercised (and which forms the State in the institutional sense of the word). The fact that the basis may change is not a reason for also changing the means.

In short,

the important thing is that one should begin to understand law no longer as a bourgeois phenomenon, but as a system of technical norms which can be employed as well by proletarian as by bourgeois to pursue certain aims which are common to them both insofar as both are social beings.[5]

Is this possible? If we admit it may be possible (as I believe), why, and in what sense, is it true? We know that the 1960 Soviet Constitution,[6] that of the post-Stalin era, if we may confine ourselves only to this, has translated this possibility into reality. For example, one can look at articles 123–8, on the equality of the rights of citizens irrespective of their nationality and race, freedom of conscience, of speech, of the press, of meetings, of union organization and, further, the right of habeas corpus, or of the 'inviolability of the person', by which 'no one can be arrested except on the order of a court or with the sanction of a public prosecutor', Art. 127, etc.[7] We have still, indeed, to grasp why this is, and its deep, complex reasons which cannot be identical with those specific to the liberal or democratic-bourgeois state, if only because those liberties and subjective rights, those technical constitutional norms, are written into the social and political records of the first socialist state, which has new, special foundations.

Hence, it seems to us essential to start with a precise distinction between the 'basis' of authority of the democratic-proletarian or socialist state, and that of the

democratic-bourgeois or liberal state, in order then to be
able to see if and how, when the basis is changed, the
'means' may change, and to what extent. Consequently, we
may postpone to the end of our inquiry the reply to the
above question. Meanwhile, to what extent in that
continuous 'work in progress' of politico-institutional
history are some unchanging means acceptable, even when
respective ends or bases change? It will be said: certainly,
some unchanging means are acceptable if one is dealing
with 'democratic' means for equally 'democratic' ends.
But the difficulty, not to be regarded as eliminated, is
exactly this: is 'modern democracy' an unequivocal term?
Bobbio himself uses a different term, that of 'liberal-
democracy'. And we can see increasingly clearly the
polemical reasons for this, which are directed against
Rousseau and in favour of Locke and Montesquieu, prior
to being directed against Marx and Lenin. Again, if it is
true that so-called national or 'popular' 'sovereignty' is
already a traditionally bourgeois doctrine as Bobbio says,
it is also true that its original, logical formulation is
Rousseau's, not Locke's, in that it pre-supposes the
distinction in principle between 'sovereign' and
'government' which is Rousseau's *discovery*, and not
Locke's. Locke admitted only a contract between governed
and governors, that is, between two particular bodies or
wills, and had not grasped the concept of 'general will' and
hence of 'popular sovereignty'.

As for the basis of the authority or sovereignty of the
democratic-proletarian, Soviet, state, it rests not on
bourgeois 'civil society', but on the organic proletarian
mass of the workers. Vyshinsky says: 'The essence of Soviet
authority is that the constant and sole base of all state
authority – of the whole state mechanism – is the mass
organization of precisely those classes which were
oppressed by capitalism,' and 'in this sense Soviet
authority is truly popular authority.'[8] 'Civil society', in the
historical and technical sense, is something quite different,
and the source of another authority. Vyshinsky recalls for

us, in contrast, this concept as defined for the bourgeois state by the jurist Hauriou, who says that 'the state is possible only where the nation has become *civil society*, i.e. where *political power has been separated from private property* and has acquired the features of a public power', whence 'a regime of "civil freedom" ' is 'a regime of freedom and equality established by a political organism, the State, *in order that the automatism of economic society might be able to function within the State*' (my emphasis).[9]

That is a point firmly to be grasped by the modern bourgeois jurist; namely that of the typical model (civil society) by which classical economics, from Ferguson on, has expressed the fundamental dogma of *homo oeconomicus* as *bourgeois*, *distinguished* from *homo politicus* as *citizen*. That figure had led the idealist Hegel to conclude in absolute terms that the 'citizen (as *bourgeois*) [. . .] is the *concreteness* of the representation that is called *man*' (*Philosophy of Right*, para. 190).[10] *Tout court*. This figure, on the other hand, is already criticized by the young Marx as a 'people in miniature', as '*class* edition' of the civil community (*Critique of Hegel's Philosophy of Law*, translated by della Volpe, (Rome. Editori Riuniti, 1950, p. 118)).[11]

However, the modern representative state, with its *separation of powers*, is really the state which Hauriou tells us is possible only where the nation has become 'civil society'. In other words, it is the state which is only 'an *abstraction* of that society' (civil, class),[12] as the young Marx has already observed: 'this political act is a complete *transubstantiation*'[13] or 'an ecstasy',[14] since 'in it, civil society must *completely give itself* up as civil society, as civil estate',[15] etc. And the subsequent criticism to which Marx himself already subjected the bourgeois separation of powers and representative institutions is pregnant with meaning and worth recalling:

Either: separation of political State and civil society takes place [said Marx] in which case *all* cannot *individually* share in legislative power [. . .], and the participation of civil society in the political State through *delegates* . . . is precisely the *expression* of their separation and of their merely dualistic unity [. . .]. Or, conversely: civil society is *actual* political society. In this case, [. . .] the legislative power is representation here in the sense in which *every* function is representative, in the sense in which, e.g. the shoemaker, insofar as he fulfils a *social* need, is my representative [. . .] in which every person is the representative of every other. He is here representative [. . .] because of what he is and *does*.[16]

Through this, Marx at the time of the Commune of 1871 could grasp that 'the Commune was to be a *working*, not a parliamentary, body, executive and legislative at the same time' (*The Civil War in France*).[17] And consequently Lenin could conclude in *State and Revolution* (1918) that 'representative institutions remain, but *there is no* parliamentarism here as a special system, as the *division of labour* [. . .], as a *privileged position* for the deputies'[18] (my emphasis). Now, precisely because Vyshinsky examines an economic society or society of producers which is a *real* political society, the Soviet state, he must specify (immediately after the passage quoted by Bobbio) that 'the programme of the All-Union Communist Party (of Bolsheviks) rejects the bourgeois principle of the separation of powers',[19] and that 'Soviet authority [. . .] abrogates the *negative sides* of parliamentarism, especially the separation of legislative and executive power, the remoteness of representative institutions from the masses and so on'.[20] Already here, once the basis of authority is changed, the means are *transformed*.

What is the value of enjoying *in the abstract* the highest refinements of the technique of bourgeois *public law*? One especially questions the value when one does not yet in all honesty (as I believe is the case with Bobbio himself) feel able to accept as an unchallengeable principle the Hegelian idealist, and natural law *generality*, which says, as we have seen, that *man* in his concreteness or full humanity is none other than the citizen as *bourgeois*.

Besides, it is also significant that Kelsen, the greatest living bourgeois jurist, can remark as follows regarding the imperfect democratic representation entailed by parliamentarism as division of labour: 'Legal independence of parliament from the people means that the principle of *democracy* is, to a certain extent, *replaced* by that of the *division of labour*. In order to conceal this shifting from one principle to the other, the *fiction* is used that parliament *"represents"* the people' (my emphasis).[21] This seems a faint echo of the young Marx, who started from the premiss that 'the modern [representative] state, in which "matters of general concern" and preoccupation therewith are a monopoly [of civil society!], and in which, on the contrary, [economic!] monopolies are the real matters of general concern, has invented the strange device of appropriating "matters of general concern" as a *mere form*'.[22] He continued: 'With this it has found the corresponding form for its content, which is only seemingly composed of real matters of general concern', and concluded that 'the state interest has again required actuality *formally* as the interest of the people, but it is *only* this *formal actuality* which it is to have' and 'has become a *formality*, the *haut goût* of national life, a *ceremonial*'.[23] It is the lying ceremony of popular-class-representation – a contradiction in terms. But it is first of all obvious that Kelsen's technical observation is governed by the *Rousseauan* concept of democracy – direct, anti-representative democracy – and not the *Lockean* or liberal one. 'Popular sovereignty,' says Rousseau, 'cannot be represented,' since 'it consists in essence of the general will.' To be certain that the particular will of each representative is the general will, it is necessary for the representatives to be mingled with the body of the people, but then they are no longer representatives, they are the people. Therefore, 'the deputies of the people are not and cannot be its representatives, they are only *its commissars*'.[24]

Again one touches upon the inner contrast of modern 'democracy', more or less concealed but no less profound, which reverberates – and is resolved – in the new proletarian democracy. Vyshinsky and Kelsen lend a hand to Rousseau – even if the former condemns Rousseau as 'ideologist of the radical petty bourgeoisie'[25] allowing on the other hand more than a page for Kant! – against Locke, Montesquieu and Constant.

This fertile contrast and its solution are fully brought together in Kelsen's objective analysis of Soviet democracy, that is, of the original Soviet development of the *positive* aspects of parliamentarism. The analysis is based on the 1924 constitution, but is even better suited, as regards the main aspects which concern us, to comparison with the constitution of 1936 (cf. Vyshinsky, pp. 104–496).

Given the impracticability of direct democracy in the large economically and culturally evolved States [says Kelsen, in a problematic speculation alluding to Rousseau], the effort required to establish the most regular and close contact between the popular will and the necessary representatives of the people, the *tendency to draw near to direct rule*, does not lead at once to a removal, nor even to a reduction, but rather to an unexpected overdevelopment of parliamentarism. The Soviet constitution [. . .] as against bourgeois representative democracy, shows this clearly. It replaces a single parliament [. . .] by a system of innumerable parliaments, set over each other, those *soviets* or councils, which are nothing but representative assemblies. But together with this extension of itself, parliamentarism is also intensified. From simple 'meetings of chatterers', parliaments must become in the view of modern communism, *working assemblies*. This means they must not be limited to enacting laws [. . .] but must take responsibility for their enforcement, and direct the process of the creation of the juridical order right up to the realization of their rules. Is this not simply an attempt to *democratize* the *administration* rather than the legislation? The official appointed by the bureaucracy, that is autocratically, and who has the power, within the often very extensive area laid down by the law, of imposing his will on the citizens, would be replaced by the citizen himself, who thus would become subject, not object, of the administration. On the other hand, this would be accomplished not directly but through the mediation of elected representatives. To democratise the administration is above all simply to parliamentarize it[26] (my emphasis).

The 'essential demand' already put forward by the young Marx must be compared: 'that every social need, law, etc., must be understood as *political*, that is, as determined by *the state as a whole*',[27] or in other words that 'the *democratic* element must rather be the actual element which gives to itself its *rational form* in the state organism *as a whole*'.[28] This is a demand unknown to the 'state characterized by political abstraction' (cf. above),[29] the constitutional state, with separated powers. In this state on the contrary, says Marx, there flourished the 'figure of a *formal* tendency [legislative power] opposed to another force' (executive or governmental power) and 'external' to the 'real content' which is the people not-in-miniature.[30]

One may compare this to what has already been said, and perhaps it will now be clear by what original, logical, and deep impulsion the thought and practice of communism can develop modern democracy, integrating, along with the substance of the Rousseauan problematic of popular sovereignty and direct democracy, the positive technical substance of the Lockean problematic of parliamentarism. Certainly the dominant direction given by that impulse is supplied by the Rousseauan, democratic one: the demand for *egalitarian liberty*. Just such a rapid examination of this last and the different liberal demand, or that of '*civil*' or individualist *liberty*, is now needed to draw together, if possible, the precise and conclusive meaning of the *democratic synthesis* towards which Soviet proletarian democracy is tending. This is an essential examination, which should show us the deep economic, moral, cultural, historical ends of which the progressive (socialist) proletarian-Soviet order is none other than the fitting instrument.

Civil liberty is obviously the liberty of the members of 'civil society' in its historical and technical sense. This is the liberty of capitalist, bourgeois producers, guaranteed politically by the separation of powers, and in a primary manner by the legislative-representative power, whose historical origin is the 'parliamentary' claim of the

'natural' liberties of the individual against the royal-
absolute government. It consists of free economic
initiative, of the security of (bourgeois) property, and
personal liberties among which are those of thought,
religion, the press, etc. It is for the most part specifically the
liberty of a class (but see further on, 7).

The other liberty is more universal. It is the *right* of *all* to
the *social* recognition of *personal qualities and abilities*. It is the
democratic, truly universal, demand of *merit*, or of the *social*
realization of the *individual* and hence of the personality
(see 5 above). It is indeed *egalitarian liberty*, 'just' liberty, or
liberty as function of justice, and in this sense a sort of
libertas maior. Rousseau says, 'It is (clearly) against the law of
nature [that is, against reason] that a child should give
orders to an old man, that an idiot direct a wise person,
and that a handful of men gorge on luxuries while the
hungry multitude lacks the necessities of life', in the
conclusion to the *Discourse on Inequality* where, as we know,
he sets out the problem the *Social Contract* is supposed to
solve with the formula of the sovereignty of the general
will, etc.[31] And he repeats his basic conviction at the end of
the *Rêveries* in the following words, 'I thought that to be
provided with *talents* was the surest provision *against
poverty*',[32] opposed, implicitly, to the subordination and
degradation derived from poverty. On this theme, even
today, for example, the late Whitehead, as an uneasy
liberal and in tormented tones, repeats the criticism of the
phenomenon of unemployment in liberal capitalism: 'In a
time of widespread unemployment, there is a very *real
closing down* of *freedom* for everyone concerned, from the
higher executives to the lowest grade of employees. In any
industrial region of the world today, it is a grim joke to
speak of freedom. All that remains is the *phantasm of
freedom*', and 'My point is that in our economic system as
now developed there is a *starvation of human impulses*, a *denial
of opportunity*, a *limitation of beneficial activity* – in short, a *lack
of freedom*.'[33]

Now, it is primarily with the desire and knowledge to

make good the deficiency in *this* basic *liberty*, that of the possibilities of every human individual, by looking towards that egalitarian liberty inhibited by the liberal-capitalist social system, that we observe the title to the legacy of modern democracy which communism claims for itself. The rigour with which Marxism-Leninism bears in mind the Rousseauan egalitarian demand for personal merit, in the context of the division of the products of labour in communist society in the strict and specific sense, is proved and completed in the above framework.

7

This is how Lenin in *State and Revolution* sums up and subscribes to the idea set out by Marx in the *Critique of the Gotha Programme* in this respect:

'*Equal* right' [of each to an *equal* share of the product of labour] [. . .] is *still* a 'bourgeois right' which, like every right [in the technical and historical sense of the term] *implies inequality*. Every right is an application of an *equal* measure to different people who in fact are not alike, are not equal to one another. That is why 'equal right' is a violation of equality and an injustice. In fact, everyone having performed as much social labour as another, receives an equal share of the social product [. . .]. But, people are not alike: one is strong, another is weak: one is married, another is not: one has more children, another has less and so on.' And the conclusion Marx draws is: 'With an equal performance of labour, and hence an equal share in the social consumption fund, one will in fact receive more than another, one will be richer than another, and so on. To avoid all these defects, right would have to be unequal rather than equal.' The first [socialist] phase of communism, therefore, cannot yet provide justice and equality: differences, and unjust differences in wealth, will still persist, but the *exploitation* of man by man will have become impossible because it will be impossible to seize the *means of production* – the factories, machines, land, etc. – and make them private property. [. . .] The vulgar economists [. . .] constantly reproach the socialists with forgetting the inequality of people and with 'dreaming' of eliminating this inequality.

Such a reproach, as we see, only proves the extreme ignorance of the bourgeois ideologists.

Marx not only most scrupulously takes account of the inevitable inequality of man, but he also takes into account the fact that the mere conversion of the means of production into the common property of the whole of society (commonly called 'socialism') *does not remove* the defects of distribution and the inequality of 'bourgeois right' which *continues to prevail* so long as the products are divided according to the amount of labour performed [. . .]. And so, in the first phase of communist society (usually called socialism) 'bourgeois right' is *not* abolished in its entirety, but [. . .] only in proportion to the economic revolution so far attained, i.e. only in respect of the means of production [. . .]. However, it persists as far as its other part is concerned; it persists in the capacity of regulator (determining factor) in the distribution of products and the allotment of labour among the members of society. The socialist principle 'He who does not work shall not eat', is *already* realised; the other socialist principle, 'An equal amount of products for an equal amount of labour, is also *already* realized'[1] [cf. article 12 of the 1960 Soviet constitution: '[. . .] In the USSR the principle of socialism is in force from each according to his ability, to each according to his labour'][2] But this is not yet communism, and it does not yet abolish 'bourgeois right', which gives unequal individuals, in return for unequal (really unequal) amounts of labour, equal amounts of products. [. . .] Marx continues [and concludes]: 'In a higher phase of communist society, after the enslaving subordination of the individual to the division of labour and with it also the antithesis between mental and physical labour has vanished, after labour has become not only a livelihood but life's prime want, after *the productive forces have increased with the all-round development of the individual, and all the springs of co-operative wealth flow more abundantly* – only then can the narrow horizon of bourgeois right be crossed in its entirety and society inscribe on its banners: From each according to his ability, to each according to his needs'[3] (the last emphasis is della Volpe's).

How can it be denied that Marxism-Leninism's meticulous attention to the problem of the economic-*proportional* recognition in truly communist *society* of the *diversity* of *individuals* and their abilities and needs expresses the continuity and development on a new historical plane of the authentic Rousseauan spirit of democracy? (on this basic point see *Clarifications*, 4).

But, on the other hand, how can one deny the continuity, also on a new historical plane, of the Lockean and Kantian liberal spirit in the first phase of communist society, or socialist (Soviet) state – and, in short, in socialist legality? This is the general question raised by Bobbio [which we left interrupted above], concerning the functionality of bourgeois technical juridical norms even for a proletarian state. To reply affirmatively and fully, it is certainly not enough to confine one's evidence to the Soviet constitutions as *facts*, among which is to be noticed the abolition of the 'rationing of (civil) liberty', now replaced by egalitarian liberty. This last is the dictatorship of the proletariat in the strict sense, according to a remark of Lenin.[4] That dictatorship, however, unless one wants to hypostasize historical events, does not in fact exclude the alternative of a peaceful assumption of power by the proletariat with the consensus of the popular majority. Hence it does not necessarily characterize the socialist revolution, whose end is what counts – the socialization of the means of production, etc. Rather, one must establish the *how* and the *why* of that abolition and relative socialist restoration of juridicial bourgeois norms, the norms of the 'state of law'.

The *how*, in particular, is provided for us in the socialist, selective restoration of the above-mentioned subjective rights or civil liberties *with the exclusion* of the right of private property in the means of production. This right has historically revealed itself as anti-economic, anti-social and inhuman, finally degenerated into privilege. See, for example, Articles 9–10 of the Soviet Constitution where 'alongside the socialist economic system' are envisaged 'small private enterprises of peasants and artisans who are not members [of kolkhozy and cooperatives], based on personal labour and excluding the exploitation of the labour of others. . . .'[5] However, 'every kolkhoz family, apart from the basic income of the collective economy of the kolkhoz, has for personal use a small plot of land attached to the house, the dwelling, and the productive equipment established on the plot, the livestock and small agricultural implements'.[6] Also confirmed is 'the right of personal property of the citizen over the income of their labour and over their savings, over their dwelling [. . .], over goods of personal consumption and convenience, and also the right of inheritance of the personal property of citizens'.[7] Here, therefore, *is the point to which* even in this case (cf. above, for the discussion of the original synthesis of direct democracy and parliamentarism in the Soviets), the norms of the state of law are *retained* and together transformed or *revalued*, in short *renewed*, in the special economic-social-political, progressive record of a socialist state.

As for the *why*, it is sufficient to reflect that so long as the state exists, even an advanced, democratic state such as the socialist state, and so long as there is a society organized on the relationship of governors/governed, the basic principle of the state of law, that of a limit of the powers of the State with respect to the persons of its citizens, is not yet transcended. This limit can be violated only at the cost of incalculable human iniquities and suffering. One needs only to think of the prime corollary of the principle, which is habeas corpus, and of its violations in the Stalinist socialist era. In short, it is true and unexceptionable, as Bobbio says, that

it is very easy to dispense with liberalism if one identifies it with a theory and practice of liberty as the power of the bourgeoisie, but it is much more difficult to dispense with if one sees it as the theory and practice of the limits of state power [. . .], since liberty as the power to do something concerns those who are its fortunate possessors, while *freedom as non-hindrance* concerns *all* men[8] (my emphasis).

But one should in addition bear in mind the deeper reason for that truth, which is propounded in the Kantian ethical principle of 'man as end and never means' or instrument. This principle, on the other hand, has its most satisfactory, or really universal, application only in a socialist state worthy of the name (however paradoxical this seems). That is, this application is to be found only in socialist legality, and more precisely in that socialist *renovatio* (renewal) of subjective rights or civil liberties *inspired by the principle* demonstrated above, in reference to the extinction by those rights of the right of private property in the means of production, with all the human alienations this entails (see further on *Clarifications*, 3, for the *bourgeois*, contradictory application made by Kant himself in his system of the state of law).

To conclude our remarks on the socialist state and the liberal legacy it contains, one should therefore remember: 1, that in the socialist state, subjective rights are *renewed* no less than is parliamentarism (see 6 above), as well as the bourgeois economic right expressed in the norm 'for an equal share of labour undertaken, an equal share of the product' (see above). And note on this last point that socialist renewal is evident in the *social* character recognized both in labour and in the product (cf. above, the texts of Marx and Lenin). 2, that, naturally, the element which, so to speak, precipitates, transforms, renews, this liberal substance (*libertas minor*, above) into a state socialist substance, is *libertas maior*, egalitarian liberty or the democratic demand materialistically supported. 3, finally, that the state destined to extinction, according to the definitive thesis of classical Marxist-Leninist theory, is the socialist state. *This* socialist state, in that 'society of free and equal beings', disappears in properly communist society, a society without classes in which 'public functions will lose their political character and become mere administrative functions of watching over social interests'[9] (Engels, quoted in *State and Revolution*, iv, 2).[10]

As for the historic fate of the demand for egalitarian

liberty, it seems clear that this goes beyond the extinction
of the (socialist) state inasmuch as it is transferred into that
society of beings who are free because equal, or properly
communist society. Here it exhausts itself as a class
demand. And here we find also that seemingly paradoxical
characteristic which always accompanies what is present in
movement and *real* or historical development, insofar as it is
material in its basis and direction – as opposed to the false
movement of the triadic dialectic. How otherwise can we
explain the following truth, in itself only intuited, that only
'when [. . .] all the springs of *collective wealth* flow more
abundantly' will that *moral* democratic-Rousseauan ideal of
the proportional social recognition of individuals and
hence of different talents and strengths be able to realize
itself' – *realize itself* in the communist norm 'from each
according to his ability, to each according to his needs'?[11]
Further, only thus can one explain (to omit the rest) that
the really satisfactory or universal application, or
realization, of the *ethical*, pure Kantian principle of 'man as
end and never means' can take place only in a society in
which *property in the means of production* is *socialized* – and we
observe this not without surprise.

Now, this disconcerting 'paradoxical' novelty of *solutions*
that the *present*, or *experience* of the present, as we may say,
has also inherited from the *past*, is produced by the fact that
it is precisely the *present* where *historical* development is
determined. This (relative) novelty which constitutes and
characterizes real *movement* or historical development
derives from a present driven more by its *material* than its
intellectual problems, always by definition different from
those of the past and yet always themselves human.
Historical development is decided by the continual
revaluation and broadening of those past solutions of
recurring human problems which it has *selected* as more
general and closest to the universal, and hence also
homogeneous with the solution of *its* real problems for
the future. This selection is made so that among the
chronological *precedents* (see the Hegelian historical

'accidents') some, and only some, are seen to be logical and also *historical antecedents* of the present. These are thus both the *historical* present and its logical *conclusion*, or, better, it is the first because it is the second. It is clear from this that history, understood materialistically, i.e. as what it truly is, is indeed an *histoire raisonnée*. It is, though, very different from the Hegelian kind which is *too denuded* of historical 'accidents' – 'disturbances', certainly, of any preconceived rational order like that of the Hegelian dialectic which, however, claimed nonetheless to be the historical order as well. Note that Engels is often ensnared in this difficulty of Hegelianism, and that, for example, the article on *Dialectics* in the *Great Soviet Encyclopedia* is still inspired by this Engels, while Marx was seriously and fruitfully troubled by the problem of the relation of 'logical' and 'historical'.[12] This summary methodological excursus (see too the criterion of philosophy as history-science in my *Logica come scienza positiva*, (Messina-Florence: D'Anna, 1956), especially pp. 163–219 and note 75) has been enjoined on us by the foregoing considerations of political philosophy and can perhaps be useful in further clarifying them.

NOTES

Section 6

1. Rousseau, *Les rêveries du promeneur solitaire*, X (*Œuvres complètes*, 1 (Paris. Gallimard, 1959)), p. 1099.
2. Marx, *Critique of the Gotha Programme*, quoted by Lenin in *State and Revolution* (*Collected Works*, vol. 25 (London/Moscow: Lawrence and Wishart/Progress, 1964)), p. 465.
3. Engels, *Anti-Dühring* (London: Lawrence and Wishart, 1975), p. 335
4. Bobbio op. cit. (1974), pp. 158–9. Cf. Lenin, 'The proletarian revolution and the renegade Kautsky' (*Collected Works*, vol. 25, op. cit.), p. 248 (literally 'a million times' [translator]).
5. Bobbio, op. cit. (1974), pp. 154–5, 156.
6. We shall so describe, for convenience, the constitution of 1936 'brought up to date with all the amendments enacted up to the sixth meeting of the fifth session of the Supreme Soviet of the

USSR, that is, to the end of 1960' as its Italian translator, Umberto Cerroni, says: see pp. 116–33 in *Rassegna sovietica*, Rome, July–August 1961.

7. *Sbornik zakonov SSSR i ukazov prezidiuma verkhnovnogo soveta SSSR 1938–1961* (Moscow: Izvestiya, 1961), Articles 123–8, pp. 22–3 (Art. 127, p. 23).

8. A. Y. Vyshinsky, ed., *The Law of the Soviet State* (New York: Macmillan, 1948), p. 173 (Lenin, quoted from vol. 23, p. 13, Russian edn).

9. ibid., p. 19 quoting Hauriou's *The Foundations of Public Law* (Russian edn, p. 365).

10. Hegel's *Philosophy of Right*, translated by T. M. Knox (Oxford: OUP, 1942), §190, 'the burgher or *bourgeois*. Here at the standpoint of needs what we have before us is the composite idea which we call *man*' (p. 127).

11. Marx, *Contribution to the Critique of Hegel's Philosophy of Law* (*Collected Works*, vol. 3 (London: Lawrence and Wishart, 1975)), pp. 84–5.

12. ibid., p. 79 (Della Volpe's version is retranslated here).

13. ibid., p. 77.

14. ibid., p. 73.

15. ibid., p. 77.

16. ibid., p. 119.

17. Marx, *The Civil War in France* (*Selected Works*, vol. 1 (Moscow: Foreign Languages Publishing House, n.d.)), p. 519.

18. Lenin, *State and Revolution*, op. cit., p. 424.

19. Vyshinsky, op. cit., p. 318.

20. ibid., note 11.

21. Hans Kelsen, *General Theory of Law and State* (New York: Russell and Russell, 1945/1961), p. 292.

22. Marx, *Contribution*, op. cit., p. 65.

23. ibid.

24. *Du contrat social*, pt 3, Ch. xv, op. cit., pp. 429–30 (Halbwachs edition, pp. 339–40).

25. Vyshinsky, op. cit., p. 169, note 44.

26. Hans Kelsen, *La démocratie. Sa nature – sa valeur* (Paris: Receuil-Sirey, 1932) (*Vom Wesen und Wert der Demokratie* (Tübingen: 2nd edn, 1929)).

27. Marx, *Contribution*, op. cit., p. 120.

28. ibid., p. 116.

29. ibid., p. 120.

30. English version in ibid., p. 120: 'given – besides its actual content – a *formal* twist against another power (content)'.

31. Rousseau, *Discours*, op. cit., p. 194.

32. Rousseau, *Rêveries*, op. cit., p. 1099.

33. A. N. Whitehead, *Essays in Science and Philosophy* (London: Rider, 1948), p. 117 and p. 120.

Section 7

1. Lenin, *State and Revolution*, op. cit., pp. 465–7
2. Sbornik, op. cit., p. 5.
3. Lenin, op cit., pp. 467–8.
4. It is worth noting that Lenin's remark, that the dictatorship of the proletariat is imposed (when it is imposed) as a 'rationing of liberty' justified by being 'the very precious liberty of all men' has a clear meaning only in reference to the *double* aspect of modern liberty, for which see above. (As mentioned by Sidney and Beatrice Webb in *Soviet Communism*, p. 1035 (London: Longmans, 1937): 'It is true that liberty is precious – so precious that it must be rationed.') This double aspect requires that in order to safeguard the very precious liberty of and for all, to which all have a right – that is, egalitarian freedom or *libertas maior*, which concerns the enormous majority, the mass oppressed by the slavery of wage-labour and for which, therefore, civil bourgeois liberties are of value only as a semi-liberty or formal liberty – it is necessary, when it becomes unavoidable, to ration, limit, these second liberties. These constitute the lesser freedom, lesser also because it is a premiss of the State that it is always a class product, destined to fall with the fall of class. The other freedom is the heart of society without classes, or truly communist society. This criterion of the double aspect of modern liberty constantly helps us to clarify many other formulae which we find in the classics of Marxism-Leninism: for example, the basic Leninist statement which summarizes so many of Engels's writings; 'So long as the State exists *there is no freedom*' (*State and Revolution*, V, 2) (op. cit., p. 468).
5. Sbornik, op. cit., Art. 9, p. 4.
6. ibid., Art. 7, p. 4.
7. ibid., Art 10, p. 4.
8. Bobbio, op. cit., 'Libertà e potere' (p. 278, 1974 edn).
9. Lenin, op. cit., p. 437.
10. On Communist society, see the *Programme of the Communist Party of the Soviet Union* (Rome: Editori Riuniti, 1961), which contains the draft programme presented to the XXII Congress of the CPSU, in which the 'paths of development for the passage to communist society in the next twenty years' (p. 66) are indicated. For example: 'The working class is the only class in history which does not propose to make its own power eternal [. . .] (p. 101). The passage to communism means the greatest development of the liberty of the person and of the rights of Soviet citizens [. . .] The growth of

material well-being, of the cultural level, and of the consciousness
of the workers creates the preconditions for finally arriving at the
complete replacement of measures of penal justice by those of
correction and social education [. . .] The evolution of socialist
state organization will gradually lead to its transformation into a
public, communist, self-government, in which will be merged the
Soviets, the unions, the cooperatives and other mass associations
of workers. This process will involve a further development of
democracy [. . .]. The organs of planning and computation, of
economic direction and cultural development, which are today
incorporated in the state apparatus, will lose their political
character by becoming organs of social self-government.
Communist society will be a highly organized community of
working people [. . .] Historical development leads inevitably to
the extinction of the State. For the State to be finally extinct there is
required the creation both of internal conditions – the building of
a developed communist society – and of external conditions: a
final resolution in the international field of the contradictions
between capitalism and communism in favour of the latter'
(pp. 110–11) (references to Soviet edition: *Proekt: Programma
kommunisticheskoi partii sovetskogo soyuza* (Moscow: Gospolitizdat,
1961).

As for *socialist legality*, it seems to me that combined in it is the
totality of economic and social problems in their political aspect,
problems which have accumulated since the advent of the state of
law and thereafter. It combines an historical synthesis of Rousseau
and Kant (liberty as a function of equality and vice versa). Here,
the 'sovereign general will' of the former is no longer *reduced* to an
(inter-class) and bourgeois national-popular sovereignty, but
made *actual* in (workers') popular-proletarian sovereignty.

It can admit and reconcile, through its centralism (democratic
and working-class), those civil liberties (habeas corpus, etc.) of the
bourgeois 'juridical order' which are not in conflict with the
freeing of the masses, the immense majority, from wage-slavery.
Here too, on the other hand, the juridical order of the latter
(Kant), thus revived in the heart of democratic, working-class
centralism, is only in this way able to acquire the universal validity
to which it vainly aspired in its original bourgeois rigidity. In this
connection, notice: 1, that this persistence of Kantian liberalism in
a non *a priori* manner, i.e. through the historical development of
class struggles which culminates in the socialist state, is a clear
confirmation of its class foundations no less than those of Lockean
liberalism (as opposed to the late Solari's belief), even though its
rational formulation is in fact superior to Lockean liberalism and
so explains its historical vitality (see the conclusions of this

chapter). 2, that it is not credible that this Kantian liberalism, even purified and renewed in socialist legality, can 'eternally' appease man (as Solari believed with respect to the original Kantian liberalism), since it can last only as long as the state lasts, and since the state in turn is fated to be suppressed in the social self-government of communist society, for the reasons given above. (And see in addition on Kant and Rousseau the conclusions of this chapter and further, *Clarifications*, 3 and 4.)

Finally, given this, how can the socialist state still be spoken of *à propos* of 'totalitarianism' (see above I, 5, note 1)? Only the blindest class interest can account for that. However, the truth slowly begins to make headway, as one sees for example in Michel Mouskhély and Zygmunt Jedryka's *Le gouvernement de l'URSS* (Paris: PUF, 1961) where, despite hesitations, a quite precise picture of Soviet socialist legality is drawn. Let us indicate some key points. Here is the Rousseauan element: '[. . .] By establishing the control of voters over those elected, and its sanction, the *recall*, the 1936 Constitution [Art. 142 = Art. 142 of the 1960 Constitution] seems to be inspired by *Rousseau's ideas* [. . .] Since the precedent set in 1936, popular participation in legislation requires that prior to their adoption by the organs responsible all major reforms be made the object of public examination on a national scale [. . .] Meetings of vanguard workers, regularly called by the Central Committee of the party and by the government, provide another example of this collaboration of the people in the management of public affairs. If it is a matter of deciding a concrete question, preparing some proposed law, ensuring the enforcement of some decision, reference will be made to those involved themselves [. . .] One may speak, therefore, to this extent, of an *indirect participation of the masses in the legislative business* of the State [. . .] For trades unions [. . .], the collaboration goes nearly as far as sharing public power. In matters of work and wages [. . .] the State involves them in the exercise of its legislative and executive powers. Thus, the acts concerned are issued jointly by the Central Committee of the party, the Council of ministers, and the Central council of the trade unions [. . .] For the *unions, participation in legislation and administration* is thus *directly* realized [. . .] However interesting and *original* these *new forms* of *direct and semi-direct democracy* may be, they have been in operation for such little time and in so unusual a manner that one could not pass judgement on them without risk [*sic*!]' (pp. 176 ff., and see p. 175 on Art. 47). And here is the Kantian element: 'The present holders of power make every effort to *guarantee and protect the essential rights of man and citizen* [. . .] The adoption of new codes, both penal and of penal procedure [. . .], represent the happy conclusion of the stubborn struggle waged by the Khrushchev team. The results are incontrovertible: *No one can henceforth be deprived of freedom without the sanction of the procurator, no one can any longer be judged and sentenced except by the normal organs of justice'*, etc. (pp. 234 ff.).

To sum up the contrast between the Soviet present and the past (the years of the dictatorship of the proletariat) it is enough, limiting ourselves to penal law, to cite the following comprehensive judgement of Rudolf Schlesinger on Pashukanis and his famous school of jurists in the 1920s and 1930s: 'It had been a logical implication of Pashukanis' General Theory of Law that, as long as there were antagonistic classes, the Criminal Law was still needed, it was bound to be dominated by the principle of "equivalence" – or to use the current term, *taliation*. Otherwise Criminal Law, in an attempt to do justice to the individual criminal, would lose its *predictability* and its general *preventive* efficiency' (*Soviet Legal Theory* (London: Kegan Paul, 1945), p. 208) (Italian edition, *La teoria del diritto nell'Unione sovietica* (Turin: Einaudi, 1952), p. 266).

11. Lenin, op. cit., p. 468.
12. *Bol'shaya sovetskaya entsiklopediya* (1952, 2nd edn (from Engels's review of Marx's *Contribution to the Critique of Political Economy*), p. 270).

III

SOCIALISM AND FREEDOM

It is only as a member of the bourgeois parliament that one can, in the given historical conditions, wage a struggle against bourgeois society [. . .] For the conditions determining the political line of all classes in modern society you substitute your revolutionary determination.

Lenin[1]

8

A rethinking of the relations between socialism and freedom (and democracy) seems more than ever necessary today in order to orient ourselves unequivocally with respect to the national roads to socialism as indicated by reality; that is, by the existence of a world system of socialism and the subsequent possibility of peaceful competition. We can set out, bearing the above in mind, the following dialectical-historical criteria, decisive for the question of the relationships just mentioned.

First: the double face, the 'two souls', of modern liberty and democracy. These are *civil* liberty established by parliamentary democracy and expressed theoretically by Locke, Montesquieu, Humboldt, Kant, and Constant; and *egalitarian* liberty established by socialist democracy, and expressed theoretically, explicitly, by Rousseau, and implicitly by Marx, Engels, and Lenin. Civil, or correctly bourgeois, liberty is, in its historical and technical meaning, the liberty or combination of liberties of the members of 'civil society' taken as a (class) society of individual producers. It is the totality of liberties or rights of individual economic initiative, of the security of private property (in the means of production), of habeas corpus, freedom of religion, conscience, and press, etc. It can be seen that some of these rights go beyond the bourgeois state by tending towards the universal. Civil liberty comprises the following juridico-political instruments – the separation of the powers of the state, and the ordering of the legislative power as a national-representative one, etc. – or the parliamentarism of the bourgeois, liberal state.

The other liberty expresses a universal demand. It means the *right* of *every* human being to the *social* recognition of his *personal capacities* (and what human, rational being does not have these?) It is the strictly *democratic* demand of *merit*, and hence for the *right* to *guaranteed labour*, and finally for the social realization of the human individual in general, of his person. It is precisely egalitarian liberty, more than simply liberty because it is also (social) justice – really a kind of *greater* or *effective liberty*, a liberty of the broad masses. 'I thought that to be provided with *talents* was the surest provision against *poverty*',[2] Rousseau's declaration is repeated once again (and see *Clarifications*, 4). And Engels has proposed for us a '[social] existence guaranteeing to *all* the free *development* and exercise of their physical and mental faculties'.[3] The contrast between these *two souls* of modern democracy, between the two different demands for liberty, means ultimately, in political terms, the contrast between *liberalism*, or liberty without equality or (social) justice, and *socialism* or liberty with social justice, for all – egalitarian liberty in its developed form.

Second: developed egalitarian liberty – the historical-materialist method of class struggle, through the work of Marx, Engels, and Lenin, takes the place of the exhausted, spiritualistic, bourgeois method. The latter rationalist-voluntarist-abstract, humanitarian-moralistic (and thus interclass) method was that of Rousseau himself, the discoverer of the problem of egalitarian liberty and subsequent popular sovereignty. *Egalitarian liberty is developed in the first socialist state*, born in the Soviet October revolution. Here we see this egalitarian liberty as developed in the Soviet state, to take the example of Jean-Paul Sartre's judgement (which, however, does not mention the force of Rousseauan precedents).

In an interview with Jean Bedel, recorded in *Unità*, 16 July 1956, Sartre said:

[Soviet] man has the feeling of a constant and *harmonious* progression in his *own* life and in *social* life. He lives in a system of competition in equilibrium at all points. Soviet society is a society in *competition* at *all* its *levels*. [. . .] *Equality* is *not* for them a *levelling* in which each would seek to be equal to the others. It is a *mobile hierarchy* spontaneously created through labour [see Art. 118 of the 1960 constitution: 'The right to work is assured by the socialist organization of the national economy, by the continuous development of the productive forces of Soviet society,'[4] etc.] and *merit* (my emphasis; and on the completion of egalitarian liberty in real, truly communist society, see the 1961 *Programme* of the CPSU (op. cit.) and again *Clarifications*, 4.)

On the other hand, it can be seen above that *civil* liberties are *renewed* in the dialectic of the egalitarian democracy of the Soviet socialist state, or socialist legality. And one can add to what has been said earlier, for example, that by the freeing of religious belief religion is cleansed of its traditional character as 'opium of the people', with its corresponding public implications, and is once more established as a strictly private matter. Again, the individual rights of the workers are rigorously safeguarded by the unions, which in turn collaborate with state economic organizations in the legal determination of adequate and progressive amounts of personal income in wages and social services – direct democracy.

Third. The integration of civil liberties with the progressive satisfaction of egalitarian demands in the present age, the age of *new democracies* and the peaceful competition arising from the existence of a world socialist system: the new, fruitful gradualism which is required in the political struggle of the major mass parties of Europe to create *national roads to socialism*, with, for example, a new use of bourgeois parliaments as a means of realizing democratic, structural reforms, anti-monopolistic reforms, etc. 'It is only as a member of the bourgeois parliament that one can, *in the given historical conditions*, wage a struggle against bourgeois society and parliamentarism [. . .] For the *conditions* determining the political line of all classes in modern society you [Bordiga* and company] substitute your [abstract] revolutionary determination'[5] (Lenin again, in a speech given at the Second Congress of the Communist International, 2 August 1920, and still relevant).

These seem to us the main distinctions in principle, set out as guides to practice.

NOTES

1. V. I. Lenin, *Collected Works* (London/Moscow: Lawrence and Wishart/Progress, 1966), vol. 31, p. 254 (1920: address to the Comintern).
2. Rousseau, *Rêveries*, op. cit., p. 1099.
3. Engels, *Anti-Dühring* (London: Lawrence and Wishart, 1975), p. 335.
4. Sbornik, op. cit., p. 21.
5. See note 1.

* Amadeo Bordiga (1889–1970). Active in the foundation of the Italian Communist Party and political prisoner from 1926–30. He was a 'leftist' critic of the Comintern's policies in the early 1920s.

IV

CLARIFICATIONS

1. Rousseau and Hegel

A critical comparison between the philosophico-political legacy of Rousseau and that of Hegel, even if only partial, is highly instructive.

For example, Hegel objects to the Rousseauan criterion of 'popular sovereignty', the criterion which underlies the modern state in that it tells us that the state is the people, and that they are the real sovereign, not the head of government who is only an employee, an officer of the true sovereign, which can always recall him, dismiss him like any other official when he fails to carry out the tasks assigned to him by the sovereign. Hegel objects that 'the sovereignty of the people is one of those confused notions which are rooted in the wild idea of the people',[1] since 'the people, conceived of without its monarch, and without the corresponding organization necessarily and immediately joining together the totality, is the shapeless mass [*die formlose Masse*].' The complete position of Hegel (Hegel the eclectic) as regards this is that for him too the state is sovereign, rather than the head of government; whilst sovereignty is still monarchical, i.e. the sovereignty of the state is expressed in the *individual* monarch, the person of the prince, in royal blood. This is the 'political zoology' of which Marx was to speak in the *Critique of Hegel's Philosophy of Law*.[2]

If one adds his theory of the upper house, or house of peers, as summit of the state and 'supreme synthesis', composed as it is of *landed* owners, first-born lords and hence 'born' legislators *'without the accidental character of a popular choice'*, this involves the idealization of the type of state definable as that of the Restoration period rather than that of the English constitutional monarchy of his time. This is the exact meaning of the much vaunted 'organicism' of Hegel. It is a *conservative* organicism, and it is worth asking if such an organicism (and think of his *Sittlichkeit*, morality) would not be a remedy much worse than the evil (Rousseau's natural law 'atomism', etc.) it was supposed to cure! And the defect of the (metaphysical) method which leads to these results, as the above shows Marx grasped correctly, is that he '*present*(s) *that which is as the nature of the state*'.[3] I.e. the metaphysical idealization of things as they are, far from being able to transcend them absolutely, is uncritically subordinate to them, and hence concludes by proposing as ideal and normative a crude and undigested empiricism.

2. Liberalism and/or democracy

Worthy of note and relevant as ever are some reflections of the late Harold Laski in his fine historical essay *The Rise of European Liberalism* (see the 1950 French edition and the corresponding unpublished conclusion). The 'universal' freedom of liberalism:

But the freedom it sought had no title to universality, since its practice was limited to men who had property to defend. It has sought, almost from the outset [. . .] to confine the business of government within the framework of constitutional principle; and it has tried, therefore, fairly consistently to discover a system of fundamental rights which the state is not entitled to invade. But, once more, in its operation of those rights, it has been more urgent and more ingenious in exerting them to defend the interests of property than to protect as claimant to their benefit the man who had nothing but his labour-power to sell. It has attempted, where it could, to respect the claims of conscience [. . .]; but the scope of the conscience it has respected has been narrowed by its regard for property [. . .].'[4]

Freedom and equality in liberalism:

[. . .] It has, accordingly, always tended to make an antithesis (as a rule an unconscious one) between liberty and equality. It has seen in the first that emphasis upon individual action for which it is always zealous; it has seen in the second the outcome of *authoritarian* intervention of which the result, in its view, is a cramping of individual personality. The outcome of this is important. For it has meant that liberalism, though it has expressed itself always as universal, has, in its institutional result, inevitably been more narrow in its benefit than the society it sought to guide. [. . .][5]

Liberalism and individual freedom:

The individual liberalism has sought to protect is always, so to say, free to *purchase* his freedom in the society it made; but the number of those with the means of purchase at their disposal has always been a minority of mankind. The idea of liberalism, in short, is historically connected, in an inescapable way, with the ownership of property. The ends it serves are always the ends of men in this position. Outside that narrow circle, the individual for whose rights it has been zealous has always been an abstraction upon whom its benefits could not, in fact, be fully conferred.[6]

The compromises of liberalism:

[. . .] They [the defenders of liberalism] were ready to accept universal suffrage, [the typical social-democratic institution] but only to the point where this did not call into question the basis of the idea of bourgeois property. They were ready to accept popular education to the point where this did not involve the payment of excessive taxes, and did not threaten the union of property and power.[7]

The concession and limit of lay liberalism;

They were ready to separate the Church from the State to the point at which the decline of the power of the Church did not lead the fourth estate to doubt the right of the bourgeoisie to confuse its special privileges with the necessary foundations of society.[8]

One may complete this picture of liberalism, as dark as it is historically correct, by adding that it does not yet contain the whole truth about liberal civilization, as Laski, the

great defender of the modern state as state of law, knew
very well. That is, we wish to refer the reader back to the
historical dialectic of the socialist state, mentioned above
(II, 7) in which the civil liberties of the liberal or bourgeois
state are both negated and preserved – or *renewed*. This
means, as we know, that the historical dialectic (of socialist
legality) is the negative-positive relation of liberalism or
'parliamentary democracy' – (Laski, however, strangely
avoids the term 'democracy' in his book) – with social
democracy, or democracy in the strict sense. Alternatively,
we may say it is the negative-positive relation of civil with
egalitarian liberty. The summarizing formula of the
problem resolved by this historical dialectic could be thus
expressed: liberalism and/or democracy.

3. More on Kant, the bourgeois moralist

We have seen previously (II, 7) that the techniques, or
better the juridical principles, of the limitation of state
power, or civil liberties, are implied by the ethical principle
'man is end and never means'. So, it is of no slight interest
to examine the application of that principle by the man
who formulated it, Kant.

One has to see clearly, without blinkers, what precise
meaning it was given by Kant, who provided us with the
philosophical *system* of liberalism. One has to see how this
formula comprises the central criterion of the Kantian
system, and thus with what other criteria, more or less
compatible with it, it comes to be connected. In short, we
must see how – and how limited and partial – this ethical
formula is made to appear when taken in its precise
historical meaning; this so-solemn formula, remember,
which is the very same as the (liberal) Kantian formulation
of the human *personality*.

'Only man considered as person, that is as the subject of
practical reason,' Kant said in the *Theory of Virtue*, the
second part of the *Metaphysics of Morals*, 'is above any price'

or is not equivalent to the '*market price*' of '*commodities*'. 'As such [. . .] he must be considered as not simply the means of other human individuals [. . .] but rather as end in himself: and thus he possesses a dignity (an absolute internal value)', which is precisely 'his [human] dignity (personality)'.[9]

However, this formulation of the *dignity* or absolute value of the human individual presupposes the following conception of the *freedom* of this same individual, according to Kant – and it is, we shall see, inseparable from it. That is, it presupposes the conception of that *a priori*, presocial, anarchic, abstract freedom, which is peculiar to the doctrine of '*natural rights*' or natural law theory (see above, I, 1, 2, 3), and which culminates in the following logical imperatives/postulates of the Kantian *Theory of Right* (the first part of the above-mentioned *Metaphysics*). (a) One 'enters society (if you cannot avoid it) with others so that in it each may preserve what [already] belongs to him'; (b) 'Innate equality is the same as independence [. . .], and yet it is the quality man has to be his own master.'[10]

Now, it is incontrovertible that these formulae (or formulae like them) have been the criteria which have led modern (bourgeois) consciousness to victory against the historical forms of despotism and privilege with which it found itself struggling for self-expression. It should be sufficient to reflect on everything which *in fact* was understood and contained, as regards the rights of the individual, in the intellectual formula of a '*conservation*' and defence of what was judged to be rooted in the nature of the individual human being as such. This was held to run from the right of unlimited private property and freedom of economic enterprise and trade, to the rights of conscience, etc. But it seems to us no less incontrovertible – *pace* the last surviving natural law theorists and idealists – that these criteria were found to undergo historical wear and tear, like all criteria, and to show in their own systematic expression and structure the signs of their historical limits, together with those of their historical fruitfulness. Hence they are not '*eternal*', contrary to what their proponents believe.

We see at once in these remarks by Kant the delimiting, class character of privileged dignity (for a human minority) which the above-mentioned '*dignity*' of the human individual, or his capacity to be end and never a simple means, *implicitly* possesses. One is dealing here, it seems, only with a comparison of value between manual or external activity, and moral or rational activity – the latter, in consequence, spiritually the most internal. 'Skill,' says Kant, 'and diligence in labour have a market value [. . .]; on the other hand, fidelity to promises, benevolence from principle (not from instinct), have an intrinsic worth.'[11] That is, they have '*virtues*' and concern the '*dignity*' of man. Thus, explaining the implicit meaning, the *labouring* man as such has only a '*price*', is a '*commodity*', and has no intrinsic value: he is simply a means and not an end in himself, in short, he does not have the '*dignity of mankind*', is not a '*person*', has no personality.

And yet, insofar as he is a *man*, the individual labourer cannot help having intrinsic '*dignity*' and '*value*', etc., for the Christian, natural law theorist, Kant. It is unnecessary to dwell on this – at least in the sense that nothing prevents the worker as man, in the spirit of the system, being himself the '*subject of practical reason*' and hence 'virtuous', on occasion, and a '*person*' with all that entails. But that does *not* concern him as a *worker*. This is also true not only in the abstract but in the concrete as well, i.e. for a worker who lives in a human community, as worker-citizen, as we shall see.

This is the antinomy, the radical, *historical* contradiction which will sweep away this pre-eminently bourgeois system of rights and virtues. As for Kant's proposed resolution of such a profound difficulty, one finds it there spelled out (but obviously deceptively, if it cannot be glimpsed by idealist and liberal moralists), in the most telling place for a difficulty of that kind. That is, it is to be found in the theory of legislative power, more precisely in that of electoral law, where the labourer, the fourth estate, the proletariat, inevitably returns on stage.

Given that 'only the ability to vote provides the qualification of the citizen', and that 'this ability, however, presupposes the independence of such people in society, since they wish to be not only a part of the community but also members of it, that is, a part which acts in accordance with its own will in communication with the others', Kant concludes that 'this latter quality necessarily makes the difference between active and passive citizen, though the concept of passive citizen seems to be in contradiction with the definition of the concept of a citizen in general.' But, 'The following examples,' he thinks, 'can help to remove this difficulty. The apprentice employed by a manufacturer; the servant (not the servant in the service of the state); the pupil [. . .]; all women [. . .]; the woodcutter I employ in my yard [. . .]; the private tutor [. . .]; the peasant who works on a daily basis for the farmer, and people of this kind – are simple dependents of the state, since they must be given orders or protected by other people, and in consequence they possess no civil independence', i.e. 'they lack civil personality.'[12]

At this point, Kant glimpses that the '*difficulty*' is not really 'removed' but only exposed, for he continues:

his dependence on the will of others and this [civil] inequality are not, however, at all contrary to the freedom and equality of these same individuals as men, who all together make up a people; also it is only on the basis of their conditions that this people can become a state and enter into a civil constitution. In this constitution, however, not all can claim the right to vote by the same title, that is, the right to be citizens and not merely associates. For the fact that that they can demand to be treated as passive parts of the state by all the others, according to the laws of natural freedom and equality, does not allow them to derive therefrom the right of acting as active members of the state itself, nor that of organizing the state or cooperating in introducing laws, but only that right, whatever the character of the positive laws voted in by those who have the right to vote,

that these laws must not be contrary to the natural laws of liberty
and the subsequent equality of all members of the people in the
capacity to raise themselves from their passive state to an active
one.[18]

In short, the citizen-labourer, in Kantian terms, is
recognized as a citizen with all the rights, *all* the *human*
prerogatives of the situation. He has, too, the independence and dignity and being-an-end-in-oneself and
possession *also* of a *civil* personality – but only *potentially*,
through his chance of *'promotion'* from labourer to
bourgeois. In other words, the labourer-citizen is a
chrysalis of a man who develops fully, when he does
develop, in the training-ground of class enterprise, that of
bourgeois, civil, society, which is given its law in the state of
'law' or liberal state (i.e. law in its abstract purity, since the
real history of the state of law, difficult and even dramatic,
is then bound in reality to contaminate that purity with
egalitarian, and clearly democratic, implants like universal
suffrage). Alternatively, the labourer has no choice but to
remain a chrysalis of a man, or, if one prefers, a pupil or
minor, with all that implies. Thus a classic liberal like
Benjamin Constant can say in his *Political Principles*, with a
cynicism unknown indeed to the straightforward Kant,
that if 'political rights' are recognized in the 'non-
possessors', rights 'which you do not owe them', 'these
rights in the hands of the greatest number will unfailingly
serve to invade property'.[14]

In other words, the solemn ethical formula of man-as-
end, etcetera, taken in its original Kantian usage, in essence
lacks universality, as it is only applicable to the bourgeois
individual. This individual alone is *in any sense a person* (as
Marx reminds his opponents in the *Manifesto*: 'You must,
therefore, confess that by 'individual' you mean no other
person than the bourgeois, than the middle-class owner of
property',[15] so Kantian doctrine itself frankly confirms
this).

Now let us compare the resulting *positive*, liberal
formulation of *civil inequality* by Kant, which is the heart of

the theory of electoral law and all its above-mentioned presuppositions, with the *negative*, critical, formulation of the same by the egalitarian, democratic, Rousseau. 'It follows again,' says the conclusion of Rousseau's *Discourse* on inequality, that moral [civil] inequality, *legitimated only by positive law*, is contrary to the law of nature [i.e. law according to reason] each time it does not coincide in the same proportion with physical inequality [i.e. immediate individual inequality of 'strength', 'health' and 'talent' or of personal merits and capacities]'.[16] Note that on this conclusion rests the argument of that *'fundamental problem'* the *Social Contract* has to solve, according to which the *'social* pact' sets up thereby a 'moral [civil] and legitimate equality' of such a kind among men that they, 'though being unequal in strength and talent, *all* become equal by convention and of right'.[17]

Here, quite apart from the Rousseauan electoral theory of the *direct* exercise, in assemblies, of *popular* sovereignty derived from the social contract, the *universal* equality in law of the citizens of the democratic Rousseauan state is quite clear, as opposed to the liberal-Kantian state. The former is a universal, juridical equality where *every* human individual must, without distinction, be recognized as a person, etc.

That Rousseauan, contractual, natural law, an ultimately *moralistic* outline of the problems of democracy, has been shown insufficient for their solution (see above, I, 1, 2, 3, 5, and II, 7), and been replaced by a radically different treatment and method, like the materialist ones of class struggle, etc., naturally involves another argument. And yet it remains quite true that the problematic of scientific socialism is the pursuit and development, on another historical and intellectual level, of the modern democratic, egalitarian problematic. That runs from the demand for real, social, recognition of the personal merits and potential of every human individual without distinction (against both class discrimination as well as a utopian social levelling of individuals!), to the demand for

a radically popular character of the sovereignty of the
social body (but see too *Clarifications*, 4).

Finishing with Kant, one has to point out, 1, that in its
libertarian Kantian application, or its rationalist-abstract,
systematic and exact meaning, the solemn ethical formula
of man-as-end has a *currency limited* to the world of
bourgeois man (and hence is shown to be self-
contradictory, antinomic). This indeed is its original,
real, historical-class value. 2, That, however, the socialist,
materialist conservation-innovation of those civil liberties
which are the immediate juridical corollaries of the ethical
formula in question, itself creates the possibility of a more
extended (even universal) application. This requires the
socialist abolition of the servitude of wage labour, which it
presupposes, and which gives the conservation-innovation
its substance. The formula itself is thus developed as a
value, in the legality of the socialist state, and always (a
further progression) as a class-historical value. (For the
structure of the historical dialectic implied herein, see the
methodological conclusions of II, 7.)

4. The problematic of the 'Discourse on Inequality', and its present importance

1 It must first be said that the relation of Rousseau and
Marxism, or the historical, systematic (theoretical) relation
between the (democratic) problematic of egalitarianism
and that of scientific socialism, is today still anything but
clear. This has an important influence as regards the
practice as well as the theory of socialism, if one but thinks
of the current acuteness of the traditional battle between
socialism (democracy) and liberalism. In this respect, the
classics of Marxism leave us in some confusion. Thus
Marx, in his analysis of the expropriation of the 'multitude
of small producers' by the 'great manufactories' (*Capital* I,
Ch. 30) makes use of Rousseau the (moralistic) critic of
economic subjection in a passage from the *Discours sur
l'économie politique* which, in Marx's quotation, runs literally

as follows: 'I shall allow you, *says the capitalist*, the honour of serving me, provided you give me the little you have left for the trouble I take to give you orders.'[18] But, to go no further, in *On the Jewish Question*, Marx shows us in a hurried quotation only as an ('excellent') picture of the bourgeois 'abstraction of political man', precisely that famous passage of the *Social Contract* (II, vii)[19] in which there is much more. Here Rousseau's attempt to integrate the *natural man*, abstractly independent, in the social body is quite clear.

This involves the transformation of the individual-whole, or solitary individual in nature (see above, I, 1, 3), into the individual-part, the *citoyen* or *man in his civil state*, or, in short, *homme social*:

He who would dare undertake to institute a people must feel himself in a condition to change human nature, so to say; to transform each individual, who by himself is a perfect, solitary whole, into a part of a larger whole from which this individual may receive in some manner his life and being; to alter the constitution of man in order to strengthen it; to substitute a partial and moral existence for the physical and independent existence we have all received from nature.[20]

This, of course, does not remove the fact that the democratic, (egalitarian) Rousseauan spirit may live again, re-armed, even in the following anti-bourgeois and socialist conclusion of the *Jewish Question* itself: that the '*social* emancipation of the Jew is the *emancipation of society from Judaism*', i.e. from the class egoism of the Jew.[21]

As for Engels, his stated position regarding Rousseau and the egalitarian problematic is essentially contradictory because, on the one hand, Engels maintains (in *Anti-Dühring*, intro. 1, I, 10 and the Vorarbeiten) that 'the "*contrat social*" of Rousseau came into being, and only could come into being, as a democratic bourgeois republic',[22] – with the related consequence of the utopian, levelling egalitarianism of a Babeuf, etc. So too, if it is the case that 'especially since the French bourgeoisie, from the great revolution on, brought civil equality to the forefront, the French proletariat has answered blow for blow [the *proletarische Konsequenzzieherei*] with the demand for social, economic equality,' and that 'in both cases the real content of the proletarian demand for equality is the demand for the *abolition of classes*',[23] it is nonetheless true that the principle of equality is 'essentially *negative*'. From this, 'because of its *lack of positive content*', it can as well be adapted to a great revolution like that of 1789–96 as to 'the later blockheads engaged in manufacturing systems'.[24]

Yet, on the other hand, he concludes (in op. cit., I, 13) an attempt at analysis of the egalitarian system of Rousseau, that is, of some themes of the *Discours sur l'origine et les fondements de l'inégalité parmi les hommes* (themes as: what are for the poet gold and silver but for the philosopher 'iron and corn, which have civilized *man* [singular, *individual* humans] and ruined the human race'),[25] with some 'dialectical' considerations, like the following:

Each new advance of civilization is at the same time a new advance of inequality [. . .] And so inequality once more changes into equality; not, however, into the former natural inequality of speechless primitive men, but into the higher equality of the social contract. It is the negation of the negation. Already in Rousseau, therefore, we find not only a line of thought which corresponds exactly to the one developed in Marx's *Capital*, but also, in details, a whole series of the same *dialectical* terms of speech as Marx used: processes which in their nature are antagonistic, contain a contradiction; transformation of one extreme into its opposite; and finally, as the kernel of the whole thing, the negation of the negation, etc.[26]

These are considerations which, though conceding *too much* to Rousseau through Engels's bad habit of looking for the greatest number of precedents for the historical-materialist dialectic, and placing Rousseau alongside Marx also as regards *method* – ('a line of thought which corresponds') – then concede too little in reality, by submerging the specific egalitarian (anti-levelling), problematic in a play of schematic and generic antitheses and syntheses of inequality and equality. This reveals the Hegelian residue often present in Engels's formulations of the historical-materialist dialectic.

2. Let us now concern ourselves with raising the specific problematic of Rousseauan egalitarianism, by going beneath the surface. This egalitarianism is, we repeat, anti-levelling egalitarianism *par excellence*, and we shall be surprised by the extent of the legacy left by Rousseau to scientific socialism – not the utopian variety. Also surprising is the historical non-exhaustion, in the French revolution, of the Rousseauan democratic problematic, or its dialectical-historical vitality – even though this is not to be reduced to generic antitheses-syntheses of the Hegelian-intellectualist kind, as in the Engels quoted above. Let us start by following the line of the problematic in the *Discours sur l'inégalité*.

Rousseau, as we see, starts with the *distinction* of two types of *inequality* which we shall rediscover at the end, after the whole problematic-moral excursus through hypothetical prehistory ('the primitive state' [the 'pure state of nature'] [. . .] a state which [. . .] has perhaps never existed [. . .] One must undertake research [. . .] on this subject [. . .] only for the sake of hypothetical or conditional reasoning'),[27] and through the history of humanity, of which the body of the *Discours* consists. But this distinction we shall at the last find *resolvable* again in a *harmonious unity* in an ideal or rational society (one *not* 'contrary to natural law'), whose specific problematic will certainly be the object of the *Social Contract*, but without our being able in fact to say that it is thereby exhausted in it, as we shall see.

Rousseau says:

It is of man that I must speak [. . .] I conceive of two kinds of inequality in the human species: one which I term *natural* or physical, because it is established by nature, and which consists in the difference of ages, health, bodily strength and the qualities of mind or spirit; the other, which one can call *moral* or *political* [or also: 'inequality by *institution*'] because it rests on a

kind of convention, and is established, or at least legitimated, by
the agreement of men. This consists of the different privileges
which some enjoy to the detriment of others: as by being richer,
more respected, more powerful than the rest, or even by making
themselves obeyed by them.[28]

The egalitarian Rousseau, indeed, will finish up by
reconciling or synthesising inequalities – these two basic
kinds of inequality.

What does this mean? He denies that at present one may
'see if there is really no essential connection between these
two inequalities':[29] what then? Listen, however, to the
reason he gives, still at the start of his inquiry, for this
denial:

For this would mean asking, in other words, if those who give
orders are necessarily better than those who obey, and if the
strength of body or mind, wisdom or virtue, are always present
in the same individuals in proportion to their power or wealth, a
question which is possibly a good one for slaves to toss around,
with the sympathy of their masters, but which is not useful for
free and reasonable beings, who are looking for truth. Exactly
what, then, is the purpose of this *Discours?* To point out the
moment in the *progress of things* when, law taking over from
violence, *nature* was subordinated to *law*.[30]

That is, given the conditions of the epoch of triumphant
absolutism in which he found himself beginning his
inquiry, there was no choice but to deny any rational,
necessary, connection between the two inequalities – in
other words, between human nature and law, individual
and society – unless one wished to flatter tyrants by
admitting that he who has political power or wealth *must*
necessarily be *worth more* than he who obeys or is poor.
There remained only to seek in historical progress the
origins and meaning of the present submission of nature
(the human individual) to the law, postponing to the
conclusion of the inquiry the reply to the question
contained in the original full title of the *Discours*, '[. . .]
whether it ['inequality among men' or 'inequality by

institution'] is authorized by natural law',[31] i.e. by reason –
and hence postponing any value judgement on the final
relation of the two inequalities.

  Now, historical-moral research reveals the following
truths. 1. The 'picture of the real state of nature', and that
of 'natural freedom', shows 'how *inequality, even natural
inequality*, is far from having in this state as much reality and
influence as our authors claim' (cf. Hobbes).[32] For, 'if one
compares the enormous diversity of upbringings and styles
of life found in the different orders of civil society with the
simplicity and uniformity of animal and savage life, [. . .]
one will see how the *difference between man and man* must be
much *less in the state of nature than in society*, and how much
natural inequality must increase in the human species
through inequality by institution.'[33]

2. It is thus that 'natural inequality spreads forth
imperceptibly alongside that [for example] of combination
[exchange]; and that the differences between men [. . .]
become more perceptible, more permanent in their
effects'.[34] And: 'so here are [. . .] all natural qualities put
into force, the rank and destiny of each one established not
only through quantity of goods and the ability to give
service or harm, but on their mind, beauty, strength or
presence, on *merit* or *talent*' '*personal qualities* being the *origin
of all* the others').[35]

  It is also true, however, that 'once it had been seen that it
was useful for one alone to have subsistence for two,
equality disappeared, property was introduced, labour
became necessary and [. . .] one soon saw poverty sprout
and grow along with the crops'.[36] It is also true that with
'such origins, society and laws irreparably destroyed
natural liberty, fixed the law of property for ever, and that
of [moral or political, or institutional] inequality [. . .],
and [. . .] from then on subjected the whole human race to
labour, to servitude and to poverty'.[37] In short, '*all further
progress* has been in appearance both steps towards the
perfection of the *individual* and, in reality, towards the

degeneration of the *species*' (see above: [. . .] and '*ruined* the human *race*'). Yet again, '*wealth, nobility* or rank, *power* and *personal merit*, being the chief distinctions [or "kinds of inequality"] by which one is measured in society [. . .], the *agreement* or *conflict* of these *different* forces is the surest indication of a state *well* or *badly* set up'.[38] This means that in a well-constituted state 'the *ranks* of the citizens should be regulated [. . .] according to the *real* services ["*proportional* to their *talents* and their *strengths*"] which they give to the state'.[39]

3. It follows that

inequality, being almost non-existent in the state of nature, draws its strength and growth from the development of our faculties and the progression of the human mind, and finally becomes established and legitimate by the institution of property and the laws. It follows again that *moral inequality*, legitimated only by positive law, is *contrary to natural law* [to reason] *each time it does not coincide in the same proportion with physical inequality* [natural inequality, of strength and merits, or personal differences between men] – a distinction which sufficiently clarifies what one should think of that kind of inequality which is found among all civilized peoples; since it is clearly contrary to the law of nature [i.e. against reason] [. . .] that a child should give orders to an old man, that an idiot direct a wise person, and that a handful of men gorge on luxuries while the hungry multitude lacks the necessities of life.[40]

Here is the answer, implicitly in the affirmative but with reservations, to the question in the original title of the work – whether, that is, correct discipline of the civil, social order (inequality amongst men) can be authorized by natural law, reason. The reply contains an answer inasmuch as it tells us that the social rank of each citizen (inequality *between* men) must be formalized on the basis of services rendered by him to society *in proportion* to his *personal* merits and *personal conditions* (inequality *of* men), whereby eventually the *two inequalities are reconciled*, irreconcilable though they appeared in the problematic beginning. Thus, this means that the solution to the problem of an effective universal equality requires that equality should not so much be reconciled with, as rather conditioned by, the (social) recognition of the *potentialities or freedoms of all* without distinction. It tells us too, in other words, that *equality is a proportional synthesis of inequalities*, of the two types of inequality – moral or political inequality by institution or 'between' men, and inequality 'of' men, or natural inequality, etc.

But this resolving reply implies and involves the theory of a *new society* since it is evident that the above *recognition* on which the institution of equality depends can only be *social*. This is not only because in fact it presupposes, as we have seen, the regulation of the question of 'rank' or civil order, but also and above all because *'distributive justice'*, as he concludes in the last note to the *Discours*, *'would be opposed* even *to that rigorous equality* of the *state of nature*, if that should be practicable in a civil society'.[41] From this we draw out the deepest meaning of the famous protest against those who do not understand him: 'What then! Must societies be destroyed [. . .]? This is a conclusion after my opponents, who I should like to warn, as much as leave them with the shame of drawing it'[42] – in a note to the *Discours*. This protest can to some extent refer also to those who speak, like the late Groethuysen, of a 'duality of ideals' in Rousseau.*

4. It has been seen earlier in the argument (II, 7) how Marxism-Leninism takes note of Rousseau's egalitarian claim for recognition of every merit and personal condition, by means of the distribution of the products of labour in a real, truly communist society (leaving aside the question of the exact historical knowledge of Marxism-Leninism in reaching this conclusion).

Here one can reassert that the reconstructive analysis of the authentic, basic line of the problematic of the *Discours* (as a whole) abundantly bears out the connection

* See the bibliographic note at the end of *Clarifications*, p. 103.

previously established between Rousseauan egalitarianism
and scientific socialism. It should be sufficient to recall the
final appeal of Rousseau to 'distributive justice', his
brilliant modern summons back to this chief Aristotelian
ethico-political category, with the aim of counterposing
the superiority of *social equality* to *natural equality* itself. The
first is based on the 'real services' rendered to society by
individuals, i.e. 'proportional to their talents and
strength', which are different, 'unequal'; while the other is
the 'rigorous' equality of the 'state of nature' which, even if
'practicable' in civil society, would turn out unjustly as a
result of its anarchic indifference to the diversity of
individuals, persons.

But now too the crux of the relation of the *Discours* and
the *Contrat* is revealed, that of their respective historical
destiny. In this regard, one must point out that the *Contrat
social* could initially offer only an egalitarian bourgeois[43]
solution to the problem of the *Discours* by reason of its
basic ethico-political, natural-law inspiration (see above,
I, 1, 3, 5, on the Rousseauan concept of the person, with his
preconceived, abstract individualism). (See too the famous
formula of the 'fundamental problem' of politics: 'to find
a form of association which can defend and protect with all
its common strength the person and goods of each
member'.)[44] At the most, it could extend its influence to the
democratic state of the Soviet republics (consider the
Rousseauan spirit of the Soviet institution of controlling
deputies by their electors, or the *recall* of the former by the
latter, which Vyshinsky forgets when he dismisses
Rousseau in a footnote as 'an ideologist of the radical petty
bourgeoisie'!).[45] Even then it extends its influence only by
a materialist-historical development of that criterion of
the *sovereign general will*, which already virtually destroys the
natural law system.

Yet the historico-problematic range of the *Discours*, on
the contrary, with its criterion of an *egalitarianism as mediator
of persons* transcends not only every egalitarian democratic-
bourgeois solution, but even the democratic-socialist one

(as still *political*: see above, II, 7). (Again, personal merits, it should be remembered, are contrasted as 'different' and 'original' as against all the other 'qualities', not only 'nobility', but also 'wealth': and cf. for example *Confessions*, 1, 'the money one *possesses* is the means of *freedom*; that which one *pursues* is that of slavery'.)[46] The problematic is finally resolved, a new historical level being postulated, in the future, egalitarian realization of scientific communism.

In other words, it appears difficult to deny that across a chasm in methods of solution, which runs from Rousseau's natural law spiritualism and humanitarian moralism on the one hand, to the historical materialism of the criterion of class struggle on the other, there remains the egalitarian problem of the *Discours*, which we can sum up in the following phrase from *La Nouvelle Héloïse*, V, 8, already analysed but inexhaustible: 'Everything depends on not destroying the natural man [i.e. the free *individual*] in adapting him to society.'[47] And it is this problem which the supreme scientific hypothesis devised by Marxism-Leninism reformulates in order to solve: that of the society of free and equal people, the classless or communist society in the strict sense.

Now, it is because this solution is so close in the country of the soviets, as we know from the *Programme* of the CPSU 'for the passage to communism in the next twenty years',[48] that the remarkable relevance of the *Discourse* is due.

Thus the *proletarian* (egalitarian) *consequential logic* (*Konsequenzzieherei*) is expressed (contrary to what Engels thought at times) in a *positive* theoretical content which has indeed been anticipated and prepared by the theorems of anti-levelling egalitarianism devised by the father of modern democracy. This can amaze, and seem ridiculous to, only those (mostly social-democrats, for example Mondolfo) who continue to interpret the Rousseauan message on human personality and freedom one-sidedly and in a 'juridical' (that is, natural law) sense, as in Lassalle's time. These people reduce the connection between Rousseau and socialism, we repeat, to a formal appendix of the *Declaration of the Rights of Man and Citizen*. By so doing, the completed historical consumption of natural law theory, including Rousseau's, in the great bourgeois revolution, is forgotten. So, they are unmindful of that basic, endless, need – also in Rousseau – for the social realization of every human individual with his irreplaceable merits and needs. This is the (democratic) demand for a *universal* and also *mediating* equality of *persons* which goes far beyond (formal!) bourgeois equality and its worn-out *self-justifications*, which are the dogmas of the eternal law of nature.[49]

Finally, at the conclusion of this investigation, we cannot pass over the structural differences between the two modern liberties, the *egalitarian* and the *civil*. For the first, as we have seen, is resolved in a universal *social* equality, mediating persons, and the second in a *political* equality of all before the law (especially if we consider the totality of *essential* civil liberties, or rather those reduced to the essential by the abolition of the privilege of private property in the means of production, insomuch as they re-enter socialist legality). This means, in other words, that the first freedom, which can be expressed as the freedom of each to be a person or develop their individual human capacities in life, in its full realization, transcends the state in general. It also transcends, therefore, the socialist state, and is truly made real in communist society with its *economic infra-structure* sufficient to the purpose (a paradoxical fate, as we know, for that freedom conceived primarily by the spiritualistic, humanitarian, and hence inter-class moralism of Rousseau!).

The second freedom, which can be expressed as freedom as non-hindrance of the individual by state power, has no *raison d'être* save in and for the state, and is destined to be suppressed with the state. Thus one understands better why the first liberty is called *major* and the second *minor*. But, on the other hand, one should bear in mind that these two freedoms are harmonized only in the legality of the socialist state – freedoms so different as may be demonstrated by any of their respective, customary, formulas. For the first, for example, we might quote the formula of *freedom of the human possibilities of every individual*, and for the other *freedom as state non-impediment of every individual*. That is, only in this type of state is that sharp contradictoriness, which afflicts the whole history of modern freedom and democracy, resolved. It is resolved precisely in its *renovatio*, or reduction to the human essence of the second freedom in the heart of the expansion of the first (through democratic workers' centralism).

Hence, in (Soviet) socialist legality the demand for freedom-as-function-of-equality, or *libertas maior*, and the demand for equality-as-function-of-freedom, or *libertas minor*, are in harmony. This is a formula in which its progress and positive, resolving conclusion is also demonstrated, though it is still linked with the initial, critical, negative phase of the present inquiry. Notice above, I, 1 and 3, the argument against the abstract-individual conception of an equality-as-function-of-freedom-*but-not-also-vice-versa*, and the demand made for the necessity of *reciprocity*. This is accomplished by showing us the meaning and *logical-historical* way in which the realization of that reciprocity (i.e. of freedom-as-function-of-equality-or-justice) implies, in addition, the validity of equality-as-function-of-freedom. This positive, resolving conclusion described above is not meant to be the definitive result or ultimate solution, precisely because we are dealing with a result which has, it is true, normative, ideal meaning, but at the same time possesses an historical, and class, meaning. Hence, it is a conclusion destined to be perfected or transcended in due course in communist society, which by definition is beyond classes, and beyond their corresponding antinomies and historical-intellectual deficiencies.

5. Systematic recapitulation

The final implications of the previous investigation are as follows:

1. The socialist (scientific) demand for the emancipation of the proletariat by means of class struggle is the development which resolves the democratic (Rousseauan) demand for an egalitarian freedom, or freedom of equals. (Scientific socialism does not grow like a mushroom).

2. It is true that the socialist criterion of labour as a right (before being a duty) of everyone is not explained in this universal meaning and value if labour be considered as the attribute and moral force (and weapon) of a single class, the proletariat. But it can be explained if it be considered as the attribute and instrumental moral force of everyone without distinction, whereby each realizes his personal capacities, his merits, and in short makes himself both person and free (through egalitarian freedom, or freedom of equals insofar as it makes all equal, and still remains freedom). *Merit-labour*: this, consequently, is an *axiological binomial*, indissoluble and unbreakable. In its name the revolutionary proletariat truly becomes the liberator of mankind. This means, precisely, becoming the restorer of the personal merits of every individual, i.e. of the *human person tout court*.

3. Naturally, given that egalitarian liberty, if it is to be put into operation, presupposes a society which is a real society, it follows that this liberating society can only be set up and exist as a popular-sovereign body, strongly unitary and authoritative, sufficiently so that it can prevent any centrifugal movement by individuals, groups, or parasitic classes. This society is unlike a merely apparent, anarchic society, like the bourgeois, which involves the recognition of the merits, and hence the persons, only of the members of a minority – indeed, that of the bourgeoisie. Society is liberating in that the 'rank' or social position of each member is relative to the 'services' or social tasks proportional to the merits of each. Thus the individual possibilities of each are liberated and all become persons, without distinction.

This unitary society works in such a way that each member, entrusting himself to the social body as guardian of the potential of each without distinction, can find himself as free as, and more than, before. He finds himself, that is, a person, as is possible only in a society of workers. The most pregnant and mysterious, Rousseauan, political formula is thus (for historico-intellectual reasons) deciphered and revalued: '[. . .] to find a form of association which can defend and protect with all its common strength the person [omit 'and the goods'] of each member and by means of which each, uniting himself with all others, still obeys only himself and stays as free as before.'[50] Now we advance from (bourgeois) national-popular-sovereignty – the reduction of popular sovereignty to an instrument of partial egalitarian ends – to the radical popular sovereignty enshrined in the democratic centralism of the soviets or councils of the revolutionary (Bolshevik) Russian proletariat, which hence is an instrument of universal equality.

Thus, the substitution of methods capable of resolving, plus the qualitative leap of method – from that of Rousseau's moralistic, humanitarian (inter-class) politics to that of the policy of class struggle of Marx–Engels–Lenin – removes from the above Rousseauan political formula what was still highly problematic and vague about it (which was also what made it fascinating). This had resulted from the bourgeois appropriation of the original phrase and the corresponding reduction of the criterion of popular sovereignty. Finally, it gives a concrete meaning to the demand for an egalitarian freedom or, the same thing in other words, for an anti-levelling egalitarian society, promoting through its unity the personality of each of its members (without this anti-levelling character of equality there would be no egalitarian freedom). Thus scientific socialism solves the problem of egalitarian freedom (or freedom which makes all equal while remaining freedom), and the related problem of a particular society which is able to realize it – problems transmitted to it by Rousseauan democracy. This is how the working class becomes liberator of the human race, in every sense, and

succeeds also in socialist legality by assuring a permanent
validity to civil, or political, freedom through the high
egalitarian (socialist!) value placed on it.

4. In fact, in this way, every civil liberty is comparable to
a quantity which should have a multiplier no lower than
itself. This is the equal, egalitarian multiplier which
confers on any civil liberty or subjective (public) right that
degree of value which prevents its decline into privilege.
Thus *libertas maior* guarantees *libertas minor*. We should be
clear on this. If the citizen's right to the vote – a typical civil
or political freedom – had not had, right from the start, an
egalitarian importance as an instrument of social
recognition extended to the personal merits of each
member of the third estate, and hence as instrument for the
'entry' and 'rise' in social life of a new class, what value
would it have expressed as regards civil progress? And, on
the other hand, has it not so happened that the original
bourgeois distinction (still with regard to electoral law)
between 'active' citizens and 'passive' citizens (or even
between 'citizens' and 'associates', as has been seen in
Kant) caused the right to vote to decline into privilege by
reason of its anti-egalitarian character.

Thus, sooner or later, has the bourgeoisie not had to
introduce the typical (democratic), egalitarian institution
of universal suffrage, albeit with all the defensive
refinements of modern electoral technique (see the Italian
fraud law of 1953!)?* In this way, the right of private
property in the means of production is declining into
privilege, in so far as it excludes adequate social
recognition of the personal merits – hence excluding the
development of the person – of every member of the
'fourth estate', the working mass. Hence it is its lesser
egalitarian multiplier which now degrades bourgeois
property to the point where the revolutionary demand for

* The so-called 'legge-truffa', designed to give the party or party-
alliance winning an absolute majority of the popular vote 65 per cent
of the seats in the Chamber of Deputies. It was expected to favour the
governing Christian Democrats.

egalitarian or democratic freedom constantly intervenes (today, socialist democracy; yesterday, parliamentary democracy against aristocratic and ecclesiastical property, etc.).

This process of making the egalitarian multiplier equal to the corresponding civil liberties reaches its peak in the legality expected of a socialist state (worthy of the name). This is a perfect legality, in which civil liberties with a lower egalitarian multiplier are cancelled, and hence valueless; for instance, free economic enterprise and corresponding private property in the means of production. There remain only civil liberties with an equal egalitarian multiplier (among them property for personal use, envisaged by the Soviet codes). Here, the protracted disharmony between political, formal, democracy and social, substantial democracy is ended – in short, disharmony between civil and egalitarian freedom. These are disharmonies, contradictions and deficiencies which no longer concern socialist society, which presupposes the withering of the (socialist) state.

5. From the methodical point of view one may make the point that whatever the difference or the agreement, or unity, of the two modern freedoms, the civil and the egalitarian, they arise *together* only in an *historical and intellectual* (logical) dimension, according to the dialectic described above (II, 7). This means, ultimately, the application – also, and principally, in this field of political philosophy – of the principle of the practical value of theory as its sole justification (see the Marxist theses on Feuerbach). For only by proceeding from a gnoseological, experimental-historical criterion is it possible to transform the world, on the basis, that is, of a specific, scientific knowledge of it – ceasing thus to contemplate the world distortedly by means of indeterminate abstractions or hypostases.

NOTES

1. Cf. Marx, *Contribution*, op. cit., *Collected Works*, vol. 3, quoting Hegel, p. 28.
2. ibid., p. 106.
3. ibid., p. 63.
4. H. J. Laski, *The Rise of European Liberalism* (London: Allen and Unwin, 1947 (f.p. 1936)), p. 15 (French edition, (Paris: Emile-Paul, 1950), p. 13).
5. Laski, op. cit., p. 16–17 (Fr. p. 15).
6. ibid., p. 18 (Fr. p. 16).
7. ibid. (Fr. p. 270) (i.e. the new conclusion to the French edition).
8. ibid.
9. *Metaphysics of Morals* (1797), *Theory of Virtue* (*The Metaphysical Elements of the Theory of Virtue*), Bk 1, op. cit.
10. ibid., *Theory of Right* (*Metaphysical Elements of the Theory of Right*), Introduction.
11. *Fundamental Principles of the Metaphysics of Morals*, op. cit., 2nd section.
12. *Metaphysics of Morals*, *Theory of Right*, pt 2, op. cit.
13. ibid.
14. Benjamin Constant, *Principles de politique* (*Œuvres*, Paris: Gallimard, 1957), Ch. vi, p. 1147.
15. *Manifesto of the Communist Party* (*Collected Works*, vol. 6 (London: Lawrence and Wishart, 1976)), p. 500.
16. Rousseau, *Discours*, op. cit., pp. 193–4.
17. Rousseau, *Contrat social*, op. cit., p. 367 (Bk 1, Ch. ix).
18. *Capital*, 1, op. cit., note 1, p. 746 (Rousseau, *Œuvres*, 3, p. 273, op. cit.).
19. *Contrat social*, op. cit. *Œuvres* 3, p. 381; Bk II, Ch. vii; Marx, *On the Jewish Question* (*Collected Works*, vol. 3 (London: Lawrence and Wishart, 1975)), p. 167.
20. *Contrat social*, op. cit., p. 381.
21. *On the Jewish Question*, op. cit., p. 174.
22. *Anti-Dühring*, op. cit., p. 26.
23. ibid., p. 128.
24. ibid., p. 407.
25. ibid.
26. ibid., p. 167.
27. *Discours*, op. cit. (text adapted), pp. 132–3.
28. ibid., p. 131.
29. ibid.
30. ibid., pp. 131–2.

31. ibid., p. 129.
32. ibid., p. 160.
33. ibid., pp. 160–1.
34. ibid., p. 174.
35. ibid.
36. ibid., p. 171.
37. ibid., p. 178.
38. ibid., p. 189.
39. ibid., p. 223.
40. ibid., pp. 193–4.
41. ibid., p. 222, note xix.
42. ibid., p. 207, note ix.
43. In this respect, the following texts are particularly interesting, as they contain a completely *Rousseauan* comparison between the absolutism of France and eighteenth-century parliamentary England: 1. 'In England,' Saint-Preux writes to Julie in the *Nouvelle Héloïse*, II, 19, 'it is quite a different matter [. . .] because the people play a larger part in government, public esteem there is a greater means of credit'. 2. 'For that reason' – the descriptive summary of the same letter sets forth – 'he [the 'lover', Saint-Preux] prefers England to France as a place *to have his talents valued*' (see Jean-Jacques Rousseau, *Œuvres complètes* (Paris: Gallimard, 1961), vol. 2, pp. 263, 783).

Observe therefore (a) how, from Rousseau's point of view, interest in a bourgeois-democratic government (in the English manner) is determined by the wholly Rousseauan, problematic perspective of the social recognition of personal merits (of bourgeois 'parvenus'): 'Would Julie [the *noble* Julie, the *lady of quality*] decide to become the wife of a *parvenu*? In England [. . .], though custom counts for even less, perhaps, than in France, that does not hide the fact that one can *arrive* in that society by more honest paths, because the people, playing a larger part in government, public esteem, etc. (ibid.); (b) that only in this – in (bourgeois) egalitarianism which creates parvenus – there meet, and are originally in agreement, liberalism (or the demand for civil or political freedoms) and democracy (or the demand for egalitarian freedom). For this Rousseau would achieve his share of glorious responsibility in the French revolution. But be it noted on the other hand that this is only the beginning and not the limit of the historical significance of Rousseau and his democratic dynamic, precisely because of the limited character of *bourgeois* egalitarianism, transcended by the universal egalitarianism of merits (and Labour!), which is the Rousseauan soul of democracy. From this one can investigate Rousseau's criticism of the general subjection of the 'poor' to the 'rich', a criticism used for his own purposes by Marx, as seen above, or democracy itself in its most essential sense; (c) that from this may be explained the corresponding differences of the two political methods, liberal and democratic – on the one hand parliamentarism and constitutionalism as function of national-popular (bourgeois) sovereignty, and on the other direct democracy as function of a radical popular sovereignty. These two methods can be reconciled, as we have seen, only in the original social-political synthesis of (Soviet) socialist legality.

44. *Contrat social*, op. cit., p. 360.
45. Vyshinsky, op. cit., p. 169, note 44.
46. *Les Confessions*, 1 (*Œuvres complètes*, I (Paris: Gallimard, 1959), p. 38.
47. *La Nouvelle Héloïse*, op. cit., p. 612.
48. *Programma*, op. cit., p. 66.
49. A significant document in this respect, one representative of a whole historical situation of bourgeois juridical theory and practice, emerged from the following admission by a French jurist and magistrate on a 'marked difference in their very principles' between 'Western' and 'Eastern' law. 'In the West, *whether one recognizes it or not*, everything happens as if there was *above* the law what has been called "the rule of law" (as the English say), a kind of *quintessence of moral rules*, sanctioned by public authorities, of *religious origin, made law in the eighteenth century as "natural law"*, and which every nation would adapt to its particular customs, still asserting the irreducible, and universal, nature of this "*common base*". In the East, *law* is *desanctified – demystified*, one would say by preference – and reduced to its function of *regulating social relations*. It is considered *strictly linked to the form of economic production* [. . .] It is law *in the making*, like the society in which it must establish rules of conduct' (Jacques Bellon, *Droit pénal soviétique et droit pénal occidental* (Paris: Navarre, 1961), pp. 201–2: emphasis mostly mine). And naturally it detracts nothing from the 'relevant difference' of principles set out above, when Bellon then returns (in the naïve attempt to show finally 'a certain convergence between Western conceptions and Soviet conceptions of law') to the old-fashioned and self-contradictory denial of an 'absolute ideal law' as given by Duguit, author of a classic textbook of constitutional – i.e. bourgeois – law. Identical too is his recourse to the authority of the abstract sociology of Lévi-Bruhl (law as 'social activity par excellence'). Whether 'one recognizes it or not' (to repeat Bellon's phrase), is of little importance: matters are as they are described above, in the 'West'.

See in addition, on the codification of present Soviet penal law, the very interesting essay by Umberto Cerroni, with a Russian bibliography: 'The new Soviet penal codification' in *Democrazia e diritto*, January–March 1961 (year 2, no. 1) (also published in *Edizioni Giuridiche del Lavoro*, Rome, 1961) (translator), and see the relevant documents edited also by Cerroni in *Rassegna sovietica*, May–June 1961 (pp. 126–40: 'Principles of the penal legislation of the USSR and of the federated and autonomous republics', pp. 131–44: 'Principles of penal procedure in the USSR and federated republics').

50. *Contrat social*, op. cit., p. 360.

BIBLIOGRAPHICAL NOTE

For a comparison with the theses expounded above, and for their easier understanding, we mention the following authors contributing to the most recent work on Rousseau: B. Groethuysen, *J.-J. Rousseau* (Paris, 1949) (cf. above IV, 4); R. Derathé, *J.-J. Rousseau et la science politique de son temps* (Paris, 1950) (noteworthy especially on the sources of Rousseau); R. Mondolfo, *Rousseau e la conscienza moderna* (Florence, 1954) (with Mondolfo, the social-democratic interpretation of Rousseau, started by Lassalle, reaches its peak: cf. above, *passim*); J.-L. Lecercle, *J.-J. Rousseau, Du contrat social* (Paris, 1955) (the current Marxist interpretation of Rousseau, done in a very lively way); W. Chapman, *Rousseau, totalitarian or liberal?* (New York, 1956) (correct in the criticism of Talmon, etc.: 'Rousseau's 'legislator' is no charismatic leader [. . .], individual autonomy is the key to Rousseau's moral and political theory', but he finishes by confusing Rousseau's democratic politics with the politics of the most 'modern' liberalism); Jean Starobinski, *J.-J. Rousseau. La transparence et l'obstacle* (Paris, 1958) (an original, psychologico-moral and aesthetic, analysis of Rousseauan activism: see, e.g. pp. 114 ff. on *La Nouvelle Héloïse*). For less recent bibliography, it should suffice to recall for the above purpose: C. W. Hendel, *J.-J. Rousseau moralist* (London-New York, 1934) (the classic work of liberal interpretation of Rousseau, but his defence of the Rousseauan meaning of freedom lacks a sufficient distinction between democratic and civil liberties.) There are interesting remarks on Rousseau in *Lettere filosofiche di Voltaire* by C. Luporini (Florence, 1955). Of uneven interest are the Rousseau–Locke comparisons in R. Polin, *La politique morale de John Locke* (Paris, 1960). Note in addition the interesting issue (November–December 1961) of the left-wing review *Europe*, dedicated to Rousseau, directed by P. Abraham (with contributions from Guy Besse, Jean Starobinski, Henri Wallon, J.-L. Lecercle, G. della Volpe and others). For a bibliography on the remaining questions of political theory (dictatorship of the proletariat, national roads to socialism, etc.), we direct you, for the purpose

mentioned above, to the works of Palmiro Togliatti (*La via italiana al
socialismo* (Rome,   1956)),   Valentino   Gerratana   (in   *Rinascita*,
August–September 1956), Umberto Cerroni (*La prospettiva del
comunismo*, Rome, 1960) and Lucio Colletti in various newspapers and
reviews (*Mondo nuovo*, *Il contemporaneo*, etc.). As regards differences in
the structure and function of the two modern freedoms, on which see
above, the following inadvertent admission of Vittorio De Caprariis
(Turcaret) is interesting, for its very immediate and spontaneous form;
'Habeas corpus,' he says 'was no more an efficient protection [but was
it ever?] for what was then already called [in the years (1890–1920) of
the dizzying growth of American industrialism] freedom from want'
(*Una lezione americana* in *Il Mondo*, Rome, 26 December 1961). This is
interesting, even if, naturally, the solution proposed by Christian
Democracy does not find us in agreement as regards the conflict
concerning the two freedoms, which still persists between us. His
solution lies not in socialism but in a neo-liberalism (after de
Tocqueville), whose summit would be represented by an 'anti-
monopoly policy of a new type', which would lead 'to expropriation
with compensation, to what is usually called in Europe the
nationalisation of industries'. (This indeed is better than nothing, but
does not solve the problem of the conflict of the two freedoms.) Let us
finally draw attention to *Democrazia e definizione*, by Giovanni Sartori
(Bologna, 1957) (a work of almost fanatical liberal inspiration, but still
useful); to *Proprietà nel nuovo diritto* (Milan, 1954) by Salvatore Pugliatti
(in which, among other things, it is argued that 'undoubtedly the sign
[. . .] of the crisis of the institution is expressed in the descriptive
formula, generic in the highest degree and not a little ambiguous, in
which it is said that property *has* (or *is*) a *social function*'): to the *Istituzioni
di diritto pubblico* (Padua, 1960) by Constantino Mortati (where the
democratic, Rousseauan 'personalistic requirement' is highly praised in
the comment on article 1 of our constituion: i.e. that this article means
'on the one hand to challenge the pre-eminent position accorded in
previous documents to other values (like private appropriation of the
means of production) and, on the other, to assign to *labour* the function
of *supreme evaluative criterion* of the *position* that should be *attributed to
citizens in the State*, since it was held to be the *most suitable* to express the
value of the *person*, and that *creative capacity* contained in him'. Whence
'taking labour as an informative value of social ranking implies that
the *comparative title* of the *social value* of the citizen should be deduced
from his *capacities*, *not* just from social positions acquired *without merit*
by the subject who enjoys them'. Here, however, the fact that our
constitution is of 'a compromise type' is not passed over in silence, in
the sense that 'it is held to be possible to combine private freedom and
social interest, without however deriving this combination as liberal
ideology did, from "pre-constituted harmonies" but rather entrusting

it to the moderating interventions of the State'. And it is admitted, for example, with regard to the electoral law of 31 March 1953, mentioned above, that 'effectively it seems that it conflicted with more than individual opinions, that is, conflicted with the moving spirit of the whole system which tends to ensure a correspondence between the distribution of political forces within parliament and that existing in the country' (my emphases); and see the article *Democrazia* by Nicola Matteucci in the *Enciclopedia filosofica* (Venice–Rome, 1957, 1).

Appendices

1 MORE ON SOCIALIST LEGALITY[1]

1. In the *Critique of Hegel's Philosophy of Law*, Marx's major posthumously-published work written in 1843, he says, for example:

Only the French Revolution completed the transformation of the political into social estates, or changed the differences of estate into mere social differences, into differences of civil life which are without significance in political life. With that the separation of political life from civil society was completed [in contrast with feudal society]. Within society itself, however, the class difference was developed in mobile and not fixed circles, of which free choice is the principle. *Money* and *education* are the *main* criteria.[2]

With regard to these criteria of bourgeois society Marx outlines, in the *Contribution to the Critique of Hegel's Philosophy of Law. Introduction* (1844), the following related concept of '*political* revolution', or bourgeois revolution, which was already a 'utopian dream', he says, in semi-feudal Germany around 1840.

On what is a partial, a *merely political* revolution based? On the fact that a *part of civil society emancipates itself* and attains *general domination*; on the fact that a definite class, proceeding from its *particular situation*, undertakes the general emancipation. This class emancipates the whole of society, but *only provided the whole of society is in the same situation as this class*, e.g., possesses money and education or can acquire them at will.[3]

And hence, Marx implies, this class does *not* emancipate the whole of society.

Notice, too, a little further on, the conclusion on the 'role of liberator', which belongs ultimately to the proletariat as the class which, 'organizing all the conditions of human existence on the premiss of *social liberty*', not 'merely political' liberty, transcends the 'partial' or bourgeois emancipation through a 'general and human' emancipation of man.[4] (Cf. *On the Jewish Question*, 1844, etc.)

Now, is it really true, and also the whole of the truth, that the 'political' or bourgeois revolution which has set up the equality of all, of all citizens, before the law, frees only those who are in the condition of the bourgeois class, and not also the whole society as *state* – in the form of a constitutional guarantee of rights? Or, in other words, is it the whole truth that it is only, and without distinction, the 'social' revolution (which produces 'social' liberty or the free expansion of society at every level) which brings about a 'general and human' emancipation of man?

This is the major problem that scientific socialism can no longer hide from itself, as classical Marxism did. From the start, Marx remained faithful, in essence, to this drastic, one-sided critique of the bourgeois revolution. He had, however, a most acute understanding of the historical necessity of the bourgeois juridical superstructure, showing its extension into the socialist state itself in terms of the 'equal' measurement of the distribution of goods produced by social labour, that is, the 'bourgeois' economic, legal residuum, as he says in the *Critique of the Gotha Programme*, his last important theoretical work. Yet he never concerned himself to the same degree with stressing the necessity of extending in the same socialist *state* the juridical, constitutional, guarantees of each person-citizen.

It is true that the problem of the 'social' revolution absorbed him too much to permit his recognition of the substantial and unmistakable legacy of the 'political' revolution, or the length of the persistence of certain bourgeois values in the future, in the same way as he had succeeded, on the other hand, in recognizing their importance to the past, to the medieval period. The 'true secret' of the Commune of 1871, he says in *The Civil War in*

France, is really this, 'It was essentially a working class *government*, the product of the producing against the appropriating class, the *political* form at last discovered under which to work out the economic emancipation of labour.'[5] And Lenin, as everyone knows, followed him too in this, in his theory of the 'dictatorship of the proletariat' – see *State and Revolution*, where too can be found the aforementioned text of Marx, in the context of the somewhat outdated flavour of the theory of the 'destruction of the parasite state'. Lenin, for whom it should be noted, 'democracy means equality' (only *social* equality), explains how in consequence one understands 'the great significance of the proletariat's struggle for equality and of equality as a slogan . . . if we correctly interpret it as meaning the *abolition of classes*'.[6]

Now, to confront satisfactorily this major difficulty (historically developed in the last forty years), that of the relation of Marxism with a substantial bourgeois, juridical, legacy, we hold that a *not merely historical* solution is to be found in Soviet 'socialist legality'. The first step, we should say, is the necessity of solving the highly complex problem of what 'modern democracy' means, given that this difficulty, when reduced to its essence is the same as that of the relation of social democracy (and revolution) to political democracy (and revolution). It is necessary to begin with a precise demonstration of the ambiguity of the modern concepts of liberty and democracy.

2. The double aspect, the two souls, of modern liberty and democracy are *civil* (political) liberty initiated by parliamentary, or political, democracy and expounded theoretically by Locke, Montesquieu, Kant, Humboldt, and Constant; and *egalitarian* (social) liberty, instituted by socialist democracy, and expounded theoretically in the first instance by Rousseau and then, more or less explicitly, by Marx, Engels and Lenin.

Civil, or so-called bourgeois, liberty is, in its historical meaning, the liberty or totality of liberties of the members of civil society as a (class) society of individual producers. It

is the totality of the freedoms or rights of individual
economic initiative, the security of private property in the
means of production, of habeas corpus, religion,
conscience, etcetera. Whether at least some of these rights
transcend the bourgeois state insofar as they concern that
human universal which exists in any body politic in its
entirety, is the implicit problematic of our starting-point.
Civil liberty also involves juridico-political instruments –
the separation of state powers and the ordering of the
legislative power as representative of national sovereignty,
etc., or parliamentarism in the liberal, bourgeois state.

The other liberty expresses a universal, unconditional
demand (unconditional because it is meta-political). It
means the *right* of *every human* being to *social* recognition of
his *personal* capacities and potentialities. In short, it is the
genuinely and absolutely *democratic* demand for the *merit* of
everyone, and hence of his *right* to guaranteed *labour*. It is the
demand for the social realization of the human individual
in general as a person. This is indeed egalitarian liberty,
more than liberty because it is also (social) justice, a kind of
libertas maior, as liberty of the broad masses. 'I thought that
to be provided with *talents* was the surest provision against
poverty':[7] this was Rousseau's typical declaration, still
wholly valid, taken up by Engels when he proposes to us a
(social) system 'guaranteeing to *all* the free *development* and
exercise of their physical and mental faculties'.[8]

This contrasting of the *two souls* of modern democracy,
of the two modern demands for liberty, means in political
terms, in the last resort, the comparison of liberalism, or
the political system of liberty without equality or (social)
justice, with socialism or the political system of social
justice, or justice for all (egalitarian liberty in its full
development).

But, on the other hand, how can one deny the fact of the
continuity – granted, on a new historical plane – of the
Lockean and Kantian liberal spirit in the first phase of
communist society, which is that of the present Russian
socialist state, and indeed in Soviet socialist legality?

At least indirectly, the question raised by Norberto Bobbio takes us back to this fact, as regards the functionality of the 'technical juridical norms' (of bourgeois constitutional guarantees) for a proletarian state as well. Bobbio simply attempts to show the legitimacy of the 'need to invite the defenders of the dictatorship of the proletariat to consider the forms of the *liberal*-democratic regime for the value of its more refined and advanced juridical technique'. And for Bobbio, in short, 'the important thing is that one should begin to understand law no longer as a bourgeois phenomenon, but as a system of technical norms which can be employed as much by proletarians as by bourgeois to pursue certain aims common to them both in so far as both are social beings'.[9] Now, what truth remains in this need Bobbio talks of?

We know that the present Soviet constitution in the post-Stalin era, issued in 1960 (but cf. the nearly identical contribution of 1936) includes Articles 123–8 on the equality of the rights of citizens, independent of their nationality and race, on liberty of conscience, speech, press, assembly, organization of trade unions, and also the right of habeas corpus or (it states) the 'inviolability of the person', by which 'no one can be arrested except by order of a court or with the sanction of a procurator', etc.[10] However, the specific, deep, motives for this, motives which *cannot* coincide with the specific aims of a liberal or democratic-bourgeois state, remain to be seen, if only because these liberties and rights of the subject, these technical constitutional norms, are written into the social and political record of the first socialist state which has new, special foundations.

To ascertain the validity of the requirement formulated by Bobbio it is not sufficient, certainly, to cite those *facts* which comprise the Soviet constitutions under examination, in which it is almost unnecessary to draw attention first and foremost to the abolition of that 'rationing of (civil) liberty' 'in favour of (egalitarian) liberty' which, according to a remark of Lenin, typifies the dictatorship of the proletariat in the strict sense. This dictatorship nonetheless in fact does not exclude the alternative of a peaceful assumption of power by the proletariat on behalf of a consenting popular majority unless one wishes to make historical precedents absolute. Hence, this dictatorship does not necessarily typify the socialist revolution whose end, that of the socialization of the means of production, etc., is what counts. However, one must determine the *how* and the *why* of that abolition of 'rationed liberty', and of the relative *socialist restoration* of bourgeois juridical norms or norms of the 'state of law'.

The *how* is provided for us in the *selective* – insofar as *socialist* – *restoration* of the above-mentioned rights or civil liberties, *with the exception*, i.e. *of the right of private property in the means of production*, a 'right' revealed historically as anti-economic, anti-social, and inhuman, finally declining into privilege.[11] Witness, then, Articles 9–10 of the cited Soviet constitution, where 'alongside the socialist economic system' are envisaged 'small private enterprises of peasants and artisans not members' [of the kolkhozy and cooperatives, in which however, 'every kolkhoz family, apart from the basic income of the collective economy of the kolkhoz, has for personal use a small plot of land, attached to the house, the dwelling, and the productive equipment established on the plot, livestock', etc.]. (This enterprise is) 'based on personal labour *excluding the exploitation* of the labour of others', and 'the right of *personal property* of the citizen over the income of their labour and over their savings, over their dwelling [. . .], over *goods of personal consumption* and *convenience*, and also the *right of inheritance* of the personal property of citizens'.[12] And it should be added, for example, that in the restored freedom of belief, religion is cleansed of its traditional characteristic of 'opium of the people', with the accompanying interventions by public law, and reduced to a strictly private affair. Here, therefore, is the *extent to which* the norms of the state of law are *preserved* and transformed,

revalued, in short *renewed*, in the particular economic-
social-political, progressive, record of a socialist state as a
'state of *all* the people' (Khrushchev). Here too we see how
facts in their exact historical presence rectify what is still
abstract and dogmatic in the liberal optimism of the
generous 'requirement' of Bobbio, for which see above.

As for the *why* of this socialist restoration of norms of the
state of law, it should be sufficient to make the judgement
that so long as there is a state, even a democratic state
advanced to the full like the socialist state, and so long as
there is a society organized on the relation of governing
and governed, the basic principle of the state of law, that of
the limit of the power of the state regarding the persons of
the citizens, must remain. It can be infringed only at the
price of incalculable iniquities and human sufferings.
Simply think of the chief corollary of that principle – the
right of habeas corpus – and of the violations it underwent
in the Stalinist socialist period.

Now, it is unexceptionable, as Bobbio says, that

it is very easy to dispense with liberalism if one identifies it with a
theory and practice of liberty as the power of the bourgeoisie,
but it is much more difficult to dispense with it if one sees it as
the theory and practice of the limits of state power [. . . .] since
liberty as the power to achieve something concerns those who
are its fortunate possessors, while *freedom as non-hindrance*
concerns *all* men[13] (my emphasis).

But one should also bear in mind the deeper reason for this
truth which is formulated in the Kantian ethical principle
of 'man as end and never means' or instrument. This is a
principle which, on the other hand, has its most
satisfactory or truly universal application only in a socialist
state worthy of the name – however paradoxical that may
seem – only, that is, in Soviet socialist legality. It is applied
here precisely through that socialist renewal of subjective
rights or civil liberties *inspired by the principle* described
above, which resides in the abolition of one single right by
those rights – that of private property in the means of

production, together with all the human alienations which this now involves. And this is the liberal consciousness, as deep as it is original, of recent (socialist) history, bound to *take unawares* the most self-critical liberal philosopher.

3. To arrive at a conclusion regarding the bourgeois juridical legacy present in the socialist state, one must therefore remember: (1), that in the socialist system of constitutional guarantees, civil liberties are *renewed*, no less than the parliamentarism of the popular councils, soviets, or the bourgeois-economic right expressed in the norm 'for an equal share of labour accomplished, an equal part of the product'. As for this last right, it should be observed that its socialist renewal is evident in the *social* character accorded to labour and its product; (2), that the dynamic element which transforms and renews the essence of the liberal state into that of a socialist state is the egalitarian demand, materialistically grounded; (3), that, finally, the state which is destined, according to the final hypothesis put forward by classical Marxist-Leninist theory, to 'suppress itself' in that 'society of free and equal persons', which is really and truly communist society, or classless society,[14] is *this* same socialist state. Therein: 'the public functions will lose their political character and become mere administrative functions of watching over social interests' (Engels, quoted by Lenin in *State and Revolution*).[15]

On communist society, see the *Proposed Programme* presented to the XXII Congress of the CPSU, in which are indicated the 'paths of development for the passage to communist society in the next twenty years'.[16] For example:

The working class is the only class in history which does not propose to make its own power eternal[17] [. . .] The passage to communism means the greatest development of the liberty of the person and of the rights of Soviet citizens [. . .] The growth of material well-being, of the cultural level and of the consciousness of the workers creates the preconditions for finally arriving at the complete replacement of measures of penal justice by those of social education [. . .] The evolution of socialist state organization will gradually lead to its transformation into a public, communist self-government, in which will be merged the Soviets, the unions, the cooperatives and other mass associations of workers. This process will involve a further development of [social] democracy [. . .]. The organs of planning and computation, of economic direction and cultural development, which are today incorporated in the state apparatus, will lose their political character by becoming organs of social self-government. Communist society will be a highly organized community of working people. [. . .] Historical development leads inevitably to the extinction of the state. For the state to be finally extinct there is required the creation both of internal conditions – the building of a developed communist society – and of external conditions: a final resolution in the international field of the contradictions between capitalism and communism in favour of the latter.[18]

As for socialist legality, it seems to us that combined in it is a totality of the economic and social problems, in their essentially *political* sense, which have been built up since the advent of the state of law and thereafter. It combines an historical synthesis of Rousseau and Kant (liberty as a function of equality and vice versa). Here the 'sovereign general will' of the former is no longer *reduced* to bourgeois-national-popular sovereignty but made *actual* in a (workers') popular-proletarian sovereignty. It can admit and reconcile through its centralism (democratic and working-class) those civil liberties of the bourgeois 'juridical order' (habeas corpus, etcetera) which are not in conflict with the freedom of the masses, the immense majority, from wage slavery. Here too, on the other hand, the juridical order of the latter (Kant), thus revived in the heart of democratic working-class centralism, is only in this way able to acquire the universal validity to which it vainly aspired in its original, narrow, bourgeois rigidity. In this connection, notice: (1), that this persistence of Kantian liberalism in a non-*a priori* fashion is a clear confirmation of its class foundations no less than those of Lockean liberalism (as opposed to the late Solari's belief), even if indeed its rational formulation is superior to Lockean liberalism and thereby explains its (historical) vitality; (2), it is not credible that this Kantian liberalism, even thus paradoxically universalized in socialist legality, can 'eternally' appease man (as Solari believed with respect to original Kantian liberalism), since it is clear that it can last only as long as the (socialist) state lasts, which also in its turn is fated to be suppressed in the social self-government of classless, communist society, for the reasons given above.

However, this being so, how can the Soviet socialist state, or state of all the people, still be accused of 'totalitarianism'? This persistent accusation can only be explained by or derived from the blindest class interest. However, slowly the truth begins to make headway, as one can see in the recent juridical literature – for example in *Le gouvernement de l'URSS* (Paris: PUF, 1961), by Michel Mouskhély and Zygmunt Jedryka where, despite hesitations, a quite precise picture of Soviet socialist legality is given. Let us give some key points. Here is the Rousseauan element:

By establishing the control of voters over those elected, and its sanction, the *recall*, the 1936 Constitution [Art. 142 = Art. 142 of the 1960 Constitution] seems to be inspired by Rousseau's ideas [. . .] since the precedent set in 1936, *popular participation in legislation* requires that prior to their adoption by the organs responsible all major reforms be made the object of *public examination* on a national scale [. . .] Meetings of vanguard workers, regularly called by the Central Committee of the Party and by the government, provide another example of this *collaboration of the people in the management of public affairs*. If it is a matter of deciding a concrete question, preparing some proposed law, ensuring the enforcement of some decision, *reference will be made to those involved themselves* [. . .] One may speak, therefore, to this extent, of *an indirect participation of the masses in the legislative business* of the state. [. . .] For *trades unions* [. . .] *the collaboration goes nearly as far as sharing public power*. In matters of work and wages [. . .] the state involves them in the exercise of its legislative and executive powers. Thus, the acts concerned are issued jointly by the Central Committee of the party, the Council of ministers, and the Central council of the trade unions [. . .]. For the *unions, participation in legislation and administration* is thus *directly* realized (pp. 176 ff., and see, too, p. 175 on Art. 47; my emphasis).

And here is the Kantian element:

The present holders of power make every effort to *guarantee and protect the essential rights of man and citizen*, through the organs of judicial direction and through the courts and in places of detention [. . .] Invariable basic principles are applied throughout the territory of the USSR concerning civil and penal legislation and judicial procedure. 1. The *court* is *the sole institution administering justice* [. . .] No one can henceforth be deprived of freedom without the sanction of the procurator, no one can any longer be judged and sentenced except by the normal organs of justice. By losing their all-powerful position in the state, the security police loses also [. . .] the features of a political police force [. . .]; consequently, many cases which up till now came before 'courts' of police repression or were judged with extreme severity as counter-revolutionary crimes, or attacks on the inviolable socialist discipline of labour, are now considered with much more leniency by ordinary courts. 2. (There is) *participation by popular assessors in the hearing of cases in all courts; the collegial principle of courts* (is established) [. . .]. The popular assessors play an active part not only in the trial itself but in all stages of the proceedings and the judicial hearing. The opinion of each of them carries as much weight as that of the judge [. . .]. 3: *Judges and popular assessors are elected* [. . .] They can be recalled by their electors or by decision of the court. From this principle, naturally, is derived the responsibility of Soviet magistrates to present an account of their service to their electors and the right of the electors to demand these accounts periodically [. . .]. 4. *The judges are independent and are bound only by the laws.* The constitutional principle of the independence of the courts has as its indispensable corollary the independence of the judges', etc. (p. 234 ff. and see Tomaso Napolitano, *Il nuovo codice penale sovietico*, Milan: Giuffrè, 1963).[19]

To sum up: the major juridical contrast between the Soviet present and past (the years of the dictatorship of the proletariat), it is worth citing the following conclusive judgement by Rudolf Schlesinger on Pashukanis and his famous school of penal law in the 1920s and 1930s:

'It had been a logical implication of Pashukanis's *General Theory of Law* that, as long as there were antagonistic classes, and Criminal Law was still needed, it was bound to be dominated by the principle of "equivalence" – or to use the current term, *taliation*. Otherwise Criminal Law, in an attempt to do *justice* to the individual criminal, would lose its *predictability* and its general *preventive* efficiency' (*Soviet Legal Theory* (London: Kegan Paul 1945), p. 208 (Italian edition Turin: Einaudi, 1952), p. 266, my emphasis).[20]

4. At the conclusion of this investigation, one cannot resist briefly considering the dialectic of the two modern demands for liberty, the egalitarian and the civil. Socialist legality is the more advanced historical instance of this dialectic, even if with socialism the historical import of the first, and greater, demand is not ended. This demand tends to a universal *social* equality mediating *persons*, thus affecting the second through its whole history[21] until it joins a totality of *essential* civil liberties, or liberties reduced to the essentially human through the abolition of the freedom-privilege of the private ownership of the means of production (socialist legality). If that is the case, the first demand transcends the second in its full realization, and, in that, the state in general. Transcending the state in general, including the socialist state, with its classes on the one hand and on the other the person-citizens it consists of, it becomes really valid in communist society, classless and meta-political, with its *economic infrastructure* sufficient to its purpose – a paradoxical fate, or rather the *historical* fate of that freedom conceived primarily by the spiritualistic, humanitarian, and hence interclass, moralism of Rousseau!

But, on the other hand, one should bear in mind that these two freedoms, so different as shown by any of their respective formulas – for example on the one hand that of the *social freedom of the human potential of every individual*, and on the other that of *freedom as guarantee of state non-interference against each individual* – are made compatible only in the legality of the socialist state. Precisely, they are harmonized only in the *renovatio*, or reduction to the human essential, of the second freedom in the heart of the expansion of the first freedom (through democratic-workers' centralism), which resolves the contradictoriness troubling the whole history of modern freedom and democracy. Hence in socialist (Soviet) legality, the demand of liberty-as-function-of-equality or greater liberty (Rousseau), and that of equality-as-function-of-liberty or lesser liberty (Kant), co-exist simultaneously. As the (Soviet) proletariat becomes the liberator of mankind, it is by the measure that *politics* allows, allowing it too, in socialist legality, to guarantee the effectiveness of civil liberties though the sufficient egalitarian (socialist) multiplier allotted to them.

Finally, every civil liberty worthy of the name is comparable to a quantity which should have a multiplier no lower than itself. This is the *equal, egalitarian multiplier* which *confers on any freedom or civil right the degree of value which prevents its decline into privilege*. Thus, the greater freedom guarantees the lesser. We should be clear on this.

If the citizen's right to the vote – a typical civil or constitutional freedom – had not had an egalitarian significance right from its proclamation as an effect of social recognition extended to the personal merits of each member of the 'third estate', and hence as an instrument of the entry and rise in social life of a new class, what value would it have expressed as regards civil progress? And, on the other hand, has it not happened that the original bourgeois distinction (still with regard to electoral law) between 'active' citizens and 'passive' citizens, or in Kant's terms between 'citizens' and 'associates', with its excluding or anti-egalitarian character, has caused this 'right' to vote to decline into privilege? Thus, sooner or later, the bourgeoisie has had to introduce, albeit with all the refinements of modern electoral technique (see the Italian fraudulent electoral law of 31 March, 1953!), the typical egalitarian or social-democratic institution of universal suffrage.

In this way, the right of private property in the means of production is declining into privilege insofar as it excludes adequate social recognition of the personal merits – hence excluding the development of the person – of the members of the fourth estate, the propertyless working mass. Hence it is its inadequate, lesser, egalitarian multiplier which now degrades bourgeois property to that point of privilege where the revolutionary demand for egalitarian freedom constantly intervenes.

Today, it intervenes in the form of socialist democracy, as previously parliamentary democracy opposed aristocratic and ecclesiastical property, etc. The historical process of making the egalitarian multiplier sufficient to the respective civil liberties reaches its peak in the legality expected of a socialist state (worthy of the name). This is a legality in which civil liberties with a lower egalitarian multiplier are cancelled and thus made valueless – for instance, free economic enterprise and corresponding private property in the means of production. There then remain only civil liberties with an equal, egalitarian, multiplier (among them, apart from habeas corpus, etc., property for personal use envisaged in the present Soviet codes).

Hence, the tension between political and social democracy comes to an end; the tension, in short, between civil and egalitarian freedom. This tension no longer concerns communist society which presupposes the withering of the (socialist) state and with it the disappearance of classes, and thus involves the triumph of egalitarian freedom. As such it is by definition 'a society of free and equal persons' – that society whose motto is 'from each according to his ability, to each according to his needs'.[22] One may reflect on how class character remains and is manifested in the 'state of all the people', the present

Union of Soviet Republics, with its socialist legality. For example, it is demonstrated in the direct participation in legislation and administration by the workers' unions, as above, which means membership by the institution of the Soviet trade-union in the sphere of public power, rather than in the sphere of the liberties of citizens or civil liberties.

5. With the foregoing we believe we have given an implicit reply to the questions raised for a modern Marxist reader by the texts of classical Marxism, here recalled in principle. And now let us say explicitly that it is not really true, not the whole truth, that the political, bourgeois, revolution has emancipated only the bourgeoisie, but rather that it really laid the foundations – paradoxically developed in the socialist legality of the present Soviet state – of the politico-juridical emancipation of the *whole* of society *as state*, or as a society structured on the relation of governing and governed. Thus, so long as there is a state, even a proletarian state, Montesquieu's is still a true and compelling warning, inspired by the absolute monarchical government of his time, and one which can be extended in view of the foregoing to any political power, even working-class power. He warned that 'it is of sovereign importance not to destroy or degrade human nature'.[23]

In short, the emancipation of man by man, insofar as this is possible before the coming of communist society, requires and implies political as much as social freedom, or better, the first put in harmony with the second. This is the philosophical meaning of the opening declaration of a recent judgement of the Supreme Court of the USSR on 'respect for socialist legality', which says: 'The continuing consolidation of *legality* and social order and the reinforcement of the safeguarding of the *rights* of Soviet citizens are *essential conditions* for the construction of *communist society* in our country.'[24]

NOTES

1. This essay was translated as 'The legal philosophy of socialism' in *Socialist Humanism*, ed. E. Fromm (New York: Doubleday, 1965).
2. *Contribution to the Critique of Hegel's Philosophy of Law,* op. cit., p. 267. Della Volpe uses 'classes' where the English has 'estates'.
3. *Contribution to the Critique of Hegel's Philosophy of Law, Introduction* (1844), op. cit., p. 184.
4. *On the Jewish Question,* op. cit., e.g. p. 168.
5. *The Civil War in France* (*Selected Works,* vol. 1 (Moscow: Foreign Languages Publishing House, 1962)), p. 522.
6. V. I. Lenin, *State and Revolution,* Ch. 3, Section 5, pp. 430–2, Ch. 5, Section 4, p. 472 (*Collected Works,* vol. 25, June–September 1917 (London/Moscow: Progress and Lawrence and Wishart, 1964)).
7. J. J. Rousseau, *Œuvres complètes,* 1 (Paris: Gallimard, 1959), *Les rêveries du promeneur solitaire,* 10, p. 1099.
8. Engels, *Anti-Dühring* (London: Lawrence and Wishart, 1975), p. 335 (della Volpe has 'moral' for 'mental').
9. In *Politica e cultura* (Einaudi: Turin, 1955) (1974 edn, p. 156).
10. Cf. *Sbornik zakonov SSSR i ukazov prezidiuma verkhovnogo soveta SSSR 1938–1961* (Moscow: *Izvestia,* 1961). Articles 123–8, pp. 22–3. (Art. 127, p. 23.)
11. It is interesting to note that this selective, socialist restoration of civil liberties means precisely, from the legal point of view, their transfer from the sphere of 'subjective' rights to that of 'objective' law (think of the transformation of the law of property, the main 'subjective' right). This is implicit in the following remark by Hans Kelsen (*Allgemeine Rechtslehre im Lichte materialistischer Geschichtsauffassung* ('The general theory of law in the light of the materialist conception of history') in *Archiv fur Sozialwissenschaft und Sozialpolitik* '(Tübingen, 1932, vol. 66, p. 521)): 'Law, which liberal-individualist ideology takes *above all* to be *subjective* law, is transformed in the [socialist] state into a social function – which conforms to *objective* law.' (my emphasis).
12. Sbornik, op. cit., Art. 9–10, p. 4.
13. Bobbio, op. cit., p. 278.
14. Communist society, from the point of view of the greatest and most logical bourgeois jurist, quoted above – 'This society, contrasted with the state in a liberal-individualistic world view, becomes for him [Marx] a polemical concept, but with an implication clearly opposed to its origin. Society, which will transcend the state – and which nonetheless in fact will replace the state, because it will be organized in a more authoritarian manner

– is the objective, or the result, of future development [. . .] The materialist conception of history, as a theory, has not the slightest interest in maintaining the state/law dualism, given that it recognizes in both the same social functions: the guarantee of class domination within capitalist society, and for both too expects the same destiny – to be destroyed in the classless society of full communism' (Kelsen, *Allgemeine Rechtslehre*, op. cit., p. 521).

15. *State and Revolution*, op. cit., p. 437.
16. *Proekt*, op. cit., p. 66 (also Rome: Editori Riuniti, 1961).
17. ibid., p. 101.
18. ibid., pp. 110–11.
19. See note 10 to 11, 7.
20. See on this Hans Kelsen, *Allgemeine Rechtslehre* . . ., p. 482: 'Indeed, this last statement we quote above, for an eminent Russian jurist [Stushchka] shows clearly that the principle of the Marxist theory of law, as also expressed by Stushchka: "A state based on class will always have only a class justice [. . .]" – is false, or at least only a half truth [. . .]. Stushchka says that even before the laws of transitional society [or the period of passage from socialism to communism] the members of all classes are equal, which means that the organs of justice should not make any exception in the application of the laws that these same laws do not make allowance for. In this sense, the ruling class is completely, absolutely interested in justice not being a class justice. It therefore sets up the ideal of *legality* and with it that of equality before the law. "Class justice" can be termed only a method of judgement which favours the members of the ruling class *in an illegal manner*. And when this too – going against the law – works in the interest of the ruling class, one cannot speak of class justice: instead, we are really faced with the opposite of class justice. This is precisely the danger to which Stushchka refers in the practice of Soviet justice. The class-state does not necessarily involve a class justice.' See also by Kelsen: *La teoria comunista del diritto* (Milan: Comunità, 1956), especially pp. 95 et seqq. (we shall return later to his onesideness).
21. On this, the following passages containing a wholly *Rousseauan* contrast between the France of absolutism and the parliamentary England of the eighteenth century are especially significant: 1. 'In England,' Saint-Preux writes to Julie in the *Nouvelle Héloïse*, II, 19, 'it is quite a different matter [. . .] because the people play a larger part in government, public esteem there is a greater *means of credit*.' 2. 'For that reason' – the descriptive summary of the same letter sets forth – 'he [the "lover", Saint-Preux] prefers England to France as a place *to have his talents valued*' (J.-J. Rousseau, *Œuvres complètes*, vol. II, Paris: Gallimard, 1961, pp. 263, 783). Observe

therefore: (*a*) how, from Rousseau's point of view, interest in a bourgeois-democratic government (in the English manner) is determined by the wholly Rousseauan, problematic perspective of the *social recognition of personal merits* (of bourgeois 'parvenus'): 'Would Julie [the *noble* Julie, the *lady of quality*] decide to become the wife of a *parvenu?* In England, [. . .], though custom counts for even less, perhaps, than in France, that does not hide the fact that one can *arrive* in that society by more honest paths, because the people play a larger part in government, public esteem,' etc., ibid.); (*b*) that only in this – in (bourgeois) *egalitarianism* which creates parvenus – from the start political democracy and social democracy (or the demand for egalitarian freedom) may coincide, in the sense that the former is *conditioned* by the second. For this, Rousseau was to achieve his share of glorious responsibility in the French revolution. But be it noted on the other hand that this is only the beginning and not the exhaustion of the historical significance of Rousseau and his social-democratic dynamic, precisely because of the limited nature of *bourgeois* egalitarianism, by being transcended through the universal egalitarianism of merit (and labour) which is the Rousseauan soul of social democracy. Already in the *Epître à Bordes* (1740) he said: 'I *respect* the *merit* of the *lowliest* social orders.' From this one may investigate Rousseau's criticism of the general subjection of the 'poor' to the 'rich', a criticism used for his own purposes by Marx in *Capital*; (*c*), and from this may be understood the corresponding differences of the two political methods, bourgeois democratic and social democratic – on the one hand parliamentarism and constitutionalism as function of national-popular (bourgeois) sovereignty, and on the other direct democracy as function of a radical popular sovereignty. These two methods are reconciled, as we have seen, only in the original social-political synthesis of (Soviet) socialist legality, the prelude to communist society, as sketched by Marx in the *Critique of the Gotha Programme* (1875) and by Lenin in *State and Revolution* (1918) which will see the final victory of egalitarian liberty. See above, for the conclusions of this work (the triumphant return of the Rousseauan criterion of the social recognition of merit, or talents, or the capacities of each in the Marxist formula 'from each according to his capacity', etc.) and cf. further 11, 6, 7 and *Clarifications*, 4, 5, where there is a dialectical analysis, among other things, of the following comprehensive final passage of the *Discours sur l'origine et les fondements de l'inégalité parmi les hommes*: 'The *ranks* of the citizens should be regulated [. . .] according to the real *services* [*proportional* to their *talents* and their *strength*] which they give to the State' (*Discours*, op. cit., p. 223).

22. *Critique of the Gotha Programme* (*Selected Works*, vol. 2. op. cit.).

23. Montesquieu, *De L'esprit des lois* (*Œuvres complètes*) (Paris: Gallimard, 1958), vol. 2, xv, 1, p. 490.

24. *Sovetskaya giustitsiya* 9, March 1963.

2 MONTESQUIEU'S AND VOLTAIRE'S HUMANITARIANISM – AND ROUSSEAU'S

1. Let us begin with the idea of freedom in Montesquieu. According to Montesquieu, the idea of freedom which we should form is as follows: 'One should keep in mind what *independence* is, and what *freedom* is. *Freedom is the right to do everything the laws allow*; and if a citizen could do what they forbid, there would be no more freedom, since others would have this power equally.' And a few lines earlier, to establish the difference between independence and freedom, Montesquieu says: 'It is true that in democracies the people seems to do what it wishes; but *political freedom* is not at all doing that one wants. In a State, which is to say in a society where there are laws, *freedom* can only consist of being able to do what one *should* want, and *not* being forced to do what one *should not* want'.[1] This distinction is set up very significantly and justified in advance by the following conclusive announcement in the previous chapter: 'Finally, as the *people* in democracies seems to do virtually what it wants, freedom has been set up in this kind of government; and the *power* of the people has been confused with the *freedom* of the people.'[2] This, consequently, is a message, despite the fact that it shows us the strictly *political, constitutional*, bourgeois, nature of *freedom* dear to Montesquieu, that also implicitly demonstrates the corresponding nature of *equality* according to Montesquieu.

What exactly is political freedom? 'Political freedom,' says Montesquieu, 'is to be found only in moderate governments; it is there only *when there is no abuse of power*; but it is an unchanging experience that every man who has power is moved to abuse it; and that he goes on until he reaches its limit. Who would say: virtue itself [political

freedom] needs its limits! In order that power may not be
abused, things must be arranged so that *power stops power*',[3]
etc. We know well that for Montesquieu freedom exists in
the England idealized by Locke in the *Treatise of Civil
Government*, with its division of legislative, executive, and
judicial powers, and with the relative predominance of the
legislative power over the others. Its most pleasing, synthetic formula is perhaps the following: 'Political freedom
in a citizen is that peacefulness of spirit which derives from
the opinion which each has of his security; and in order to
have that freedom, the government must be such that no
citizen can be in fear of another citizen.'[4]

But we must examine what interests us most in this
political freedom – its exact social context. This is derived:
(1) from the limits in this democracy set up against the
'sovereign power' of the 'people', or 'lower people', or
'lesser people'. Thus, Montesquieu says – 'As the majority
of citizens, which has enough capability to elect others,
does not have sufficient to be elected, so in the same way
the people which has enough capacity to judge the
management of others, is not capable of managing by
itself,' . . . Hence 'what it cannot do well, it must have its
ministers do for it',[5] i.e. its magistrates. From this is drawn,
in addition, the corollary of the exclusion from the right to
vote of those who are 'in such a degraded state as to be
reputed [*sic*] not to have the slightest personal will' (this is
Montesquieu's 'exclusive thought'!). (2) From the following, typically bourgeois, distinction between *political* and
civil law:

Since men have renounced their natural independence to live
under political laws, they have renounced the natural com-
munality of goods to live under civil laws.

The first laws provide them with their *liberty; the second with
property*. One must not decide by the laws of liberty what, as we
have said, is only the governance of the city, which should only
be determined by the laws concerning property. It is a
paralogism to say that the particular good should yield to the
public good. That takes place only in the cases where there is a

question of the governance of the city, that is, the freedom of the citizen. It has no place in those cases where there is a question of property in goods, because *the public good is always that each should preserve unchanging that property* the civil laws allow him.[6]

Yet one should not forget, in addition, the following physiocratic aphorism *avant-la-lettre*, that 'countries are not cultivated by reason of their fertility, but by reason of their freedom'.[7] Hence one sees that freedom, though distinguishable from property, is in effect principally a function of it. Compare the physiocratic articles on *fermiers, grains, impôts, laboureur*, the last relating as much to the farmer as the landowner who both undertake large-scale cultivation with substantial capital, and the articles '*Homme (politique)*' by Diderot and *Liberté* by Jaucourt, all in the *Encyclopédie*.

Now, from this kind of freedom and its relevant social context, a corresponding type of equality follows.

Love of the republic, in a democracy, is the love of democracy; love of democracy is love of equality. [. . .].

Love of equality, in a democracy, limits ambition to the single desire, the single happiness, which comes from giving one's country greater service than other citizens. Citizens cannot all render it equal service; but they must all equally render service. [. . .][8] Although, in a democracy, real equality is the soul of the state, it is nonetheless so difficult to establish that an extreme exactness in this regard would not always be convenient. It is enough that one should establish a system that reduces or fixes differences at a certain point; after that, it is up to particular laws to equalize, as it were, the inequalities, by the financial obligations they impose on the rich and the relief they provide for the poor. It is only middling riches which can give or bear such kinds of compensation [. . .] Every inequality in a democracy should be drawn from the nature of democracy and the very principle of equality itself. For example, one might fear lest those people who would need continuous work in order to live be too impoverished by the magistracy, or that they should neglect their function; or that the artisans become too proud of themselves [. . .] In these cases equality between citizens can be removed in a democracy for the purposes of democracy. (Note:

'Solon excluded from public responsibilities all those of the lowest (fourth) stratum', i.e. all those who made a living by the labour of their hands.) However, it is only an apparent freedom that one removes: for a man ruined by the magistracy would be in a worse condition than the other citizens; and this same man, who would be compelled to neglect his duties, would put the other citizens in a worse condition than his own, and so forth.[9] [. . .] The principle of democracy is corrupted not only when the spirit of equality is lost, but also when the spirit of extreme equality is adopted, and when each wants to be equal to those he chooses to govern him. Then the people, unable to bear the very power it confers, wishes to do everything itself, to deliberate in the senate's place, administer the law for the magistrates, and contest all the judges.[10] [. . .] As far as heaven is from earth, so is the *real spirit of equality* from the spirit of extreme equality. The first does not at all consist in making it possible for all to govern, or that no one be governed, but in *obeying and governing one's equals*. It does not seek to have no master, but *to have only equals as masters*. In the state of nature, men are indeed born in equality; but they could not remain so. Society makes them lose this, and they *become equal again only through laws*.[11]

It is worth recalling in this regard Jaucourt's article on *Egalité naturelle* in the *Encyclopédie*, an article certainly inspired by Voltaire, as we shall see, but also by Montesquieu. Thus:

I will simply observe that it is the violation of this principle [of natural equality] which has established political and civil slavery [. . .] However, let no one wrongly imagine that from a spirit of fanaticism I should approve in a state that *chimera* of *absolute equality*, which can scarcely father an ideal republic; I speak here only of the *natural equality* of men; I know only too well the necessity of different conditions, of the levels, honours, distinctions, prerogatives, and subordinations, which must be present in every government; and I would even add that *natural* or *moral* equality is not at all opposed to them.[12]

Consequently, the equality required by Montesquieu is that *political equality* not recognized by the ancien régime, by absolute monarchy. It is the kind of equality which conforms to purely political liberty ('equal under the laws'). However, it is also the equality produced by a state (constitutional monarchy and then modern republics), in which the 'common good', as we have seen, consists only in the strict 'conservation' of 'private property', sanctified by 'civil laws'. Ultimately, this is the *real* equality of a single *class, bourgeois equality*. It is not, and obviously could not be, what we now call *social equality*, after Rousseau and Marx. As a final point, when Montesquieu asserts with regard to 'monarchical government,' that it is 'of sovereign importance not to destroy, or degrade human nature'[13] he gives clearly a strictly *juridico-political* meaning to this lofty and weighty thought, something which indeed transcends purely bourgeois interests, insofar as it expresses the principle of the non-hindrance of the individual-citizen by the state, so long as there is a state, defined as a society articulated into governing and governed. This, then, is the *liberal* humanitarianism of Montesquieu.

2. *Freedom* according to Voltaire is set out by Maxime Leroy in the first volume of his well-known *Histoire des idées sociales en France* as follows: 'We read in the *Dictionnaire philosophique*: "Liberty and property". It is the English slogan. It is better than "*Saint George and my right*", or "*Saint Denis et Mont-joie*". It is the slogan of nature.' And he adds: 'The sense of property doubles the strength of man [. . .]' And further on: 'Not all peasants will be rich, and it is not necessary that they should be. We need men who have nothing but their hands.' Here, put into a few words, is his political and social philosophy. But does summarizing it to this extent not perhaps mean misrepresenting it?[14]

I do not believe this is such a betrayal of Voltaire's political and social philosophy. Just remember some lines on the entry '*Egalité* in the same *Dictionnaire*, for example:

It is impossible, in our sorry world, for men living in society not to be divided into two classes, one of the rich who govern, the other of the poor who obey [. . .] The human race, such as it is, cannot exist without an infinite number of capable men who possess nothing [. . .] *Equality* is thus at once the *most natural thing* and the most *chimerical* [. . .] Every man has indeed – *in the bottom of his heart* – the right to believe himself *completely equal* to other men [. . .].[15]

Or simply quote the following lines from the *Dialogue entre un philosophe et un contrôleur général des finances* '. . . The populace remains always in deepest ignorance, to which the necessity of making a living condemns it, and in which the good of the state has long been believed to lie in keeping it; but the *middle class* is *enlightened.*'[16] Or, finally his anti-Rousseauan polemical tone, fiercely contemptuous in the '*Lettres sur la Nouvelle Héloïse ou Aloïsia*' –

My lord [. . .] he said [. . .] though knowing well that Jean-Jacques was only a ragged tramp, still gave him half his goods to get married, since it had happened, once upon a time, that passing through Geneva he had heard this great man speak on *equality of conditions* (Voltaire's emphasis) and conclusively prove that a watchmaker's assistant who can read and write is quite equal to the grandees of Spain, the marshals of France, the dukes and peers of England, the princes of the empire and the syndics of Geneva.[17]

Here again is Voltaire's *social scepticism*, this time expressed in Candide's manner, and in context very badly.

It is true that Voltaire's is a political and social philosophy which is generically one of freedom and bourgeois equality, and specifically a theory of the rights and duties of the *honnête homme*, the well-set up man, who is the enlightened man the bourgeois intellectual, who comes to replace, as an élite, the *honnête-homme-homme-de-qualité*, or aristocratic man, of the ancien régime. From this Voltaire's greatest glory is derived, his brilliant defence of freedom of thought and conscience (*The Calas Affair, The Treatise on Tolerance*, etc.).

To conclude, the idea of the social and political value of personal merit as against noble birth – the egalitarian criterion which would be the intellectual driving-power of the approaching revolution – for Voltaire involves only the members of the third estate, and preeminently the intellectuals. Neither for him nor, as we have seen, for the

philosophers of the *Encyclopédie*, does it have the
redeeming breath nor the rigour of the Rousseauan idea of
personal merit and talent, as shown in these extremely
simple phrases in the *Confessions*, 11: 'I entered into the vast
space of the world with assurance: my merit would fill it.'[18]
In fact, we have seen what Voltaire thought of watch-
makers' assistants who could read and write. This *social*
indifference and agnosticism is the reverse of the fine
medal struck from his moral profile, from his *enlightened*
and *tolerant* humanity, grandly bourgeois.

3. Jean-Jacques was twenty-eight when he glimpsed the
truth, the basic criterion of equality. He says in the *Epître à
Bordes*: 'There is no wisdom where poverty holds sway;
Beneath the weight of hunger, merit beaten down/Lets
virtue in a saddened heart expire [. . .]/I respect merit in
the lowest social ranks.'[19] Note how here *merit* and *virtue*
come to be connected with *hunger* and social *degradation*,
for the times an unheard-of association. Compare too La
Bruyère's maxim, with its triumphant bourgeois
inflection, 'A fine property is witness of merit [. . .]'. We
are already far from Montesquieu, Voltaire and their
colleagues. The supreme criterion of equality is
proclaimed – the *general validity* of *personal merits*. The
problem of this 'catholic' particularity, or universality, will
be posed and guided towards its resolution fifteen years
later in the *Discours sur l'origine, et les fondements de l'inégalité
parmi les hommes*.

The problem is posed in the following terms:

I conceive of two kinds of *inequality* in the human species; one,
which I term *natural* or *physical*, because it is established by
nature, and which consists in the difference of ages, health,
bodily strength, and the qualities of mind or spirit; the other,
which one can term *moral*, or *political*, because it rests on a kind of
convention and is established, or at least legitimated, by the
agreement of men. This consists of the different privileges which
some enjoy to the disadvantage of others: as by being richer,

more respected, more powerful than the rest, or even by making themselves obeyed [. . .].[20] From this exposition it follows [Jean-Jacques concludes at the end of the *Discours*, after a long excursus on human history and pre-history] that [moral or political] inequality being almost non-existent in the state of nature ['a state which . . . has perhaps never existed'] draws its strength and growth from the development of our faculties and the progression of the human mind, and finally becomes established and legitimate by the institution of property and the laws. It follows again that *moral inequality*, legitimated only by positive law, is *contrary to natural law* [i.e. to ideal law, imposed by pure reason] *each time it does not coincide in the same proportion with physical inequality* [i.e. *natural* inequality of strength and capacities, or merits]; – a distinction which sufficiently clarifies what one should think of that kind of inequality which is found among all civilized peoples; since it is clearly contrary to the law of nature [i.e. against reason], however one defines it, that a child should give orders to an old man, that an idiot direct a wise person, and that a handful of men gorge on luxuries while the hungry multitude lacks the necessities of life.[21]

Now, the solution of the original problem of establishing a 'proportional comparison' of the natural inequality of men in terms of strength and merit with their social ('moral or political') inequality, is proposed in the following terms. 'But in general,' Jean-Jacques argues towards the end of the *Discours* – 'wealth, nobility or rank, power and *personal merit* [the latter is 'the origin of all the *other* qualities'], being the chief distinctions [or 'types of inequality'] by which one is measured in society. I could show that the agreement or conflict of these different forces is the surest indication of a state well or badly set up.'[22] In fact, finally clarified in the last note to the *Discours* 'the ranks of the citizens should be regulated [. . .] according to the *real services* [i.e. '*proportional* to their *talents* and their (unequal) *strength*'] which they give to the state.'[23] This means that for Jean-Jacques the solution of the problem of an effective universal, not merely bourgeois, equality requires the unlimited, universal application of the criterion of merit, and of personal conditions. This is the merit, the qualities or capacities, which make up the human person, who as such is never bereft of them: the origin of all other (social) qualities. It requires, in other words, that a non-utopian universal equality be based on the social recognition of the unequal or different capacities and potentialities of all men, without exception.

Consequently, this solution involves the building of a new, democratic, society, antithetical to the society of privileged persons under absolutism. For it is obvious that the recognition of *each* person with his merits, essential for the establishment of an effective equality, can only be of a social nature. This is not only because (a question of fact) it consists materially in the regulation of questions of civil order (of 'rank'). It is also, and above all, of a social nature because – as question of law – '*distributive* justice', as he said at the start of the last, authoritative note to the *Discours, 'would be opposed* even to that *rigorous equality* of the *state of nature,* if that should be practicable in a civil society'.[24] See too in note ix, the following strong protest against those, the majority, who distort the real thought of Rousseau, the 'critic' of society: 'What then! Must societies be destroyed [. . .]? This is a conclusion after my opponents, who I should like to warn, as much as leave them with the shame of drawing it.'[25] Observe too the final appeal to distributive justice (the opposite of commutative justice, that of exchange), this modern summons back to the chief Aristotelian ethical and political category, with the aim of counterposing the superiority of *social* equality to *natural* equality itself. The first is based on the civil rank of each citizen, calculated according to his real services, i.e. proportional to the strengths and talents which he has given to society. The second is the perfect equality of the mythical state of nature which, if practicable in civil society, Jean-Jacques implies, would be unjust and hence self-contradictory, given its anarchic indifference to the original, different value of every human individual, every person.

Finally, one must bring out the following: 1, that *human,*

purely *moral* equality, the only kind recognized by Voltaire and the Encyclopedists, becomes for Jean-Jacques *real* equality as *social* equality, and not merely political as for Montesquieu; 2, that since the criterion of this real equality is the social recognition of the universality (catholicity) of merits, and the implicit recognition of labour, Jean-Jacques's egalitarianism is clearly non-levelling and has nothing in common with the communist-utopian egalitarianism of Morelly, Mably, and Babeuf. Remember the words in *Emile*: 'To work is therefore an indispensable duty for social man. [. . .] Every idle citizen is a petty thief.'[26] Remember too the *Nouvelle Héloïse* 'everything depends on not destroying the natural man [i.e., the free *individual*] in adapting him to society';[27] 3, that the political institutions necessary for this real, social equality naturally go beyond the framework of liberalism, of parliamentary or bourgeois democracy, and tend, in the *Contrat social*, towards a radical democracy in which (against Montesquieu) popular *power* and popular *liberty* should coincide. Regarding this, one should recall his most telling formula, that of 'find(ing) a form of *association* which can *defend and protect* with all its common strength the *person* and goods of *each* member, and by means of which each uniting himself with all, still obeys only himself and *stays as free* as before'.[28] One strips away the mystery if by such an association one means a political instrument which guarantees and assures, by its unitary sovereign power, the assertion of merits and potential of each, that is, of his *person* and his *freedom*. This takes us, *mutatis mutandis*, very far – to the class, materialist solutions of the problems of Rousseau's egalitarianism as *mediator of persons* which are found in the socialism and communism foreseen in the Marxist *Critique of the Gotha Programme* and in Lenin's *State and Revolution*.

A *truly democratic* understanding of the *human person* is hence the revolutionary legacy, still alive today, which Jean-Jacques leaves for us. The example of his *radical democratic* humanitarianism can also lend a full and rigorous meaning to the grand but one-sided *liberal* maxim of Montesquieu noted above: that 'it is of sovereign importance not to destroy or degrade human nature'.[29] Even if this inevitably complicates the meaning of this maxim and its related problems, it results from knowing that Montesquieu had and still has his share of correct reasoning. But this would eventually involve us in the problem of *socialist legality*, to which we drew particular attention in Appendix 1.

NOTES

1. Montesquieu, *De l'esprit des lois*, (*Œuvres Complètes*, 2 (Paris: Gallimard, 1958), xi, 3, p. 395.
2. ibid., xi, 2 p. 394.
3. ibid., xi, 4, p. 395.
4. ibid., xi, 6, p. 397.
5. ibid., ii, 2, pp. 240–1.
6. ibid., xxvi, 2, pp. 767–8.
7. ibid., xviii, 3, p. 532.
8. ibid., v, 3, pp. 274–5.
9. ibid., v, 5, pp. 278–9.
10. ibid., viii, 2, pp. 349–50.
11. ibid., viii, 3, p. 352.
12. Encyclopédie, vol. 5, Paris, 1755: Chevalier de Jaucourt, *Egalité naturelle*, p. 415.
13. ibid., xv, 1, p. 490.
14. Maxime Leroy, *Histoire des idées sociales en France*, vol. 1 (Paris: Gallimard, 1946), p. 71.
15. Voltaire, *Dictionnaire Philosophique*, vol. 4 (*Œuvres Complètes*, Paris: Garnier, 1878 (Kraus reprint, 1967, vol. 18))), pp. 475–7.
16. Voltaire, *Dialogues I. Un philosophe et un contrôleur général des finances* (1751) (ibid., vol. 23), p. 502.
17. Voltaire, *Lettres sur la Nouvelle Héloïse* (1761) (ibid., vol. 24) (p. 172).
18. Rousseau, *Œuvres I* (1959) op. cit., p. 45.
19. Rousseau, *Œuvres II* (1961) op. cit., p. 1131.
20. Rousseau, *Discours*, op. cit., p. 131.
21. ibid., pp. 193–4.
22. ibid., p. 189 (text adapted from GdV's translation).
23. ibid., notes, p. 223.
24. ibid., p. 222.

25. ibid., p. 207.
26. *Emile,* op. cit., iii, p. 470.
27. *La Nouvelle Héloïse*, op. cit., pt v, letter 8, p. 612.
28. *Du contrat social*, op. cit., p. 360.
29. Montesquieu, op. cit., xv, 1, p. 490.

3 THE MARXIST CRITIQUE OF ROUSSEAU

1. In the *Critique of the Gotha Programme*, quoted and discussed by Lenin in *State and Revolution* (V, 3–4), Marx says as follows:

'Equal right' [of each to the equal product of social labour] we certainly do have here [i.e. in the first phase of communism], but it is *still* a 'Bourgeois right', which like every right, *implies inequality*. Every right is an application of an *equal* measure to *different* people who in fact are not like, are not equal to one another.[1] That is why 'equal right' is a violation of equality and an injustice. In fact, everyone, having performed as much social labour as another, receives an equal share of the social products. [. . .] But people are not alike: one is strong, another is weak. [. . .] With an equal performance of labour, and hence an equal share in the social consumption, Marx concludes 'one will in fact receive more than another, one will be richer than another, and so on. To avoid all these defects, right would have to be unequal rather than equal.' The first phase of communism, therefore, cannot yet provide justice and equality [. . .]; but the *exploitation* of man by man will have become impossible because it will be impossible to seize the *means of production* [. . .] and make them private property. [. . .] The vulgar economists [. . .] constantly reproach the socialists with forgetting the inequality of people and with 'dreaming' of eliminating this equality. Such a reproach, as we see, only proves the extreme ignorance of the bourgeois ideologists.

Marx not only most scrupulously takes account of the *inevitable inequality of men*, but he also takes into account the fact that the mere conversion of the means of production into the common property of the whole of society (commonly called socialism) *does not remove* the defects of distribution and the inequality of 'bourgeois right'.[2]

Now, Rousseau in the *Discours sur l'origine, et les*

fondements de l'inégalité parmi les hommes (1755) had posed the problem of the 'inevitable' inequality *of* men in these terms:

I conceive of *two kinds* of *inequality* in the human species: one which I term *natural* or *physical*, because it is established by nature, and which consists in the differences of ages, health, bodily strength, and the qualities of mind and spirit [or inequality *of* men]; the other, which one can call *moral* or *political* [or inequality *between* men], because it rests on a kind of convention and is established, or at least legitimated, by the agreement of men. This consists of the different privileges which some enjoy to the disadvantage of others: as by being richer, more respected, more powerful than the rest, or even by making themselves obeyed [. . .] From this exposition, it follows that [moral or political] inequality [Rousseau concludes at the end of the *Discours*, after covering the whole of human prehistory and history], being almost non-existent in the state of nature ['a state which . . . perhaps has never existed'], draws its strength and growth from the development of our faculties and the progression of the human mind, and finally becomes established and legitimate by the institution of property and the laws. It follows again that *moral inequality*, legitimated only by positive law, is *contrary to natural law* [that is, to ideal law, imposed by pure reason] *each time it does not coincide in the same proportion with physical inequality* [i.e. *natural* inequality of strength and qualities, or merits] – a distinction which sufficiently clarifies what one should think of that kind of inequality which is found among all civilized peoples; since it is manifestly contrary to the law of nature [i.e. against reason], however one defines it, that a child should give orders to an old man, that an idiot direct a wise person, and that a handful of men gorge on luxuries while the hungry multitude lacks the necessities of life.[3]

But, before looking at the last implications of this famous conclusion to the *Discours*, let us see the Marxist solution to the difficulty expounded above, in the Marx–Lenin text – that, given the inequality or diversity of men, right should be not equal but unequal, a difficulty which can now be defined as of the (anti-levelling) egalitarian-Rousseauan variety.

And so, in the first phase of communist society (usually called socialism) – Lenin's text goes on – 'bourgeois right' is *not* abolished in its entirety, but only in part, only in proportion to the economic revolution so far attained, i.e. only in respect of the means of production [. . .] However, it persists as far as its other part is concerned; it persists in the capacity of regulator (determining factor) in the distribution of products and the allotment of labour among the members of society. The socialist principle, 'He who does not work shall not eat,' is already realised; the other socialist principle, 'An equal amount of [social] products for an equal amount of [social] labour', is also already realised. But this is not yet communism, and it does not yet abolish 'bourgeois right', which give *unequal* individuals in return for *unequal* (really unequal) amounts of labour, *equal* amounts of products [. . .].[4]

Marx continues and concludes:

In a higher phase of communist society, after the enslaving subordination of the individual to the division of labour and with it also the antithesis between mental and physical labour have vanished, after labour has become not only a livelihood but life's prime want, after the productive forces have increased with the all-round development of the individual, and *all the springs of co-operative wealth flow more abundantly* – only then can the narrow horizon of bourgeois right be crossed in its entirety and society inscribe on its banners: From each according to his ability, to each according to *his needs*!'[5]

And the following conclusions of Engels in *Anti-Dühring* (III, 2) are in agreement:

The possibility of *assuring for each* member of society, by *means of socialized production*, an *existence not only fully sufficient* materially, and becoming day and day more full, but an existence guaranteeing to all the *free development* and *exercise of their physical and mental faculties* – this possibility is now and for the first time here, but it is here.[6]

Let us return to Rousseau to see the solution he provides to the difficulty of establishing a *proportional comparison* between the inequality and diversity of men and inequality between them (or the whole of the civil differences set up and administered by society) – a difficulty, as shown, re-formulated by Marx and Lenin as the necessity of unequal right, given the inevitable inequality of men, and thus resolved by their scientific criterion of a communist society.

Rousseau, therefore, explains to us that 'wealth, nobility or rank, power and *personal merit* [the latter "*origin* of all the *other* qualities"] being the chief distinctions [or "kinds of inequality"] by which one is measured in society, I could show that the agreement or conflict of these different forces [i.e. personal merit and other qualities] is the surest indication of a state well or badly set up.'[7] And in fact it is finally made clear in the last footnote to the *Discours* that 'the *ranks* of the citizens should be regulated [. . .] according to the *real services* ["*proportional* to their [unequal] *talents* and their *strengths*"] which they give to the state.'[8]

This means that for Rousseau the solution of the problem of an effective universal equality (not only for the bourgeois) requires the unlimited, universal application of the criterion of merit and personal conditions. This is the 'talent' or merits (of which no human being as such is wholly bereft) as the origin of all the other (social) qualities, and also the 'strengths' of which he speaks, the very conditions of existence of the human person (age, health, etc.). It requires, in other words, an equality based on the social recognition of the unequal or different capacities and potentialities of all men, without exception.

This solution involves, therefore, the building of a new society, a democratic one, to surpass not only the society of those privileged under absolutism, but also bourgeois society itself as based in effect on the merits-rights of the possessors. For it is obvious that the recognition of *every* person, on which the institution of a real equality, for all, depends, can only be of a social nature. This follows not only because it presupposes materially, *de facto*, the regulation of questions of 'rank' or civil order, but also and above all because (as a question of law, or of value) '*distributive* justice would be *opposed* even to that *rigorous equality* of the *state of nature*, if that should be practicable in a civil society'.[9] (And cf., still in the *Discours*, the following lively protest against those, the majority, who gravely misunderstand the Rousseauan critique of society: 'What then! Must societies be destroyed, get rid of what is yours and mine, and go back to live in the forests with the bears? This is a conclusion after my opponents, who I should like to warn, as much as to leave them with the shame of drawing it.')[10]

Consider, therefore, this final appeal of Rousseau to distributive justice (the opposite, be it remembered, of commutative or exchange justice) this modern summons back to the chief ethico-political, Aristotelian category, with the aim of counterposing the superiority of *social* equality, to *natural* equality itself. The first is based on the civil rank of each citizen, calculated according to his real services, i.e. proportional to the talents and strength which he gives to society. The second is the rigorously perfect equality of the mythical state of nature, which, if practicable in civil society, Rousseau implies, would be unjust and hence self-contradictory, given its anarchic indifference to the original, different value of every human individual, every person.

From these series of texts by Lenin–Marx, Engels, and Rousseau, we can infer that the meticulous attention bestowed by Marxism-Leninism on the problem of the economic-proportional recognition by (communist) society of the inequalities or differences of individuals and their capacity and need expresses, on a new historical level, the continuity and development of the anti-levelling egalitarian thought of Rousseau. It seems difficult, in other words, to deny that across the chasm of method which separates the metaphysical idealism and humanitarian moralism, the natural-law moralism, of Rousseau on the one hand, from the historical materialism of the criterion of class struggle on the other, lies the major problem posed by Rousseau. That is, that 'everything depends on not destroying the natural man [the *free* individual] in adapting him to society'[11] (*La Nouvelle Héloïse*, V, 8), and it is this problem which the supreme scientific hypothesis of the conclusive phase of communism re-formulates in order to solve it. (This leaves aside the question, which we shall see later, of the historical knowledge Marxism-Leninism had of its debt to Rousseau's egalitarianism.)

In this context, one can conclude as follows: 1. that scientific socialism is capable of resolving by its *materialist* method the problem of an *equality* both *universal* and *mediating of persons* which was discovered by the humanitarian *moralist* Rousseau, with his egalitarian-anti-levelling conception of the human person. I.e. a social recognition of the unequal merits and potentialities of all men through their respective proportional services rendered by each to the state; 2. that, in this ultimate concern for the human person by scientific socialism, is revealed, certainly, the Christian legacy chiefly transmitted to it by Rousseau (but how changed by him!). The difference between the heir and the bestower of the legacy consists on one hand in the first's joining the value of the person and his destiny to *history*, that is, to an institution such as a sufficiently unitary society which prevents any centrifugal movement by individuals and classes who may be parasitic and exploitative of man.

The second, Rousseau, however, joins the value of the person and his destiny to an *extra-historical*, theological investiture ('I tell you, in the name of *God* that it is the *part* [i.e. the human *individual*] which is greater than the whole [i.e. than the human *race*]', *Emile*, IV).[12] And yet this can only *justify* a *partial*, *bourgeois* solution to the problem of a *social*, truly democratic, recognition of the merits and needs of each person, given that the *sacred-a priori* of the human person can justify only an *abstract*, frustrated individualism, and consequently the kind of semi-anarchic and impotent society which is bourgeois, liberal society.

2. After this, we have still to examine the conscious disposition of the founders of scientific socialism towards Rousseau and his work.

For Marx's attitude, observe the following characteristic and significant aspects.

(1) As against Hegel's conservative opinion, that 'the sovereignty of the people is one of those confused notions which are rooted in the *wild* idea of the people', Marx retorts that 'the "confused notions" and the "wild idea" are here exclusively Hegel's (the posthumously published *Critique of Hegel's Philosophy of Law* (1843).[13] And in the same work, pervaded wholly by the typical Rousseauan idea of popular sovereignty, the people 'represented' in the liberal state is defined by Marx as 'people in miniature' (as the 'estate edition' of civil society).[14]

(2) However, in *On the Jewish Question* (1844) Marx offers us only as an ('excellent') picture of the bourgeois 'abstraction of political man' the famous passage in the *Contrat social* (II, 7) in which is clearly visible the democrat Rousseau's attempt to integrate 'natural', abstractly independent, man into the social body, and thus to transform the individual-whole, or solitary individual of nature, into the individual-part which is the citizen, social man. Rousseau in fact says: 'He who would care to undertake to institute a people must feel himself in a condition to change human nature, so to say; to transform each individual, who, by himself, is a perfect, solitary whole, into a part of a larger whole, from which this individual may receive in some manner his life and being', etc.[15] Thus is explained (though not justified) how, making a judgement of Rousseau as a political writer at the beginning of the *Introduction* (1857), (published posthumously) and in the *Grundrisse* (1857–8, published posthumously), Marx sees in Rousseau only the worshipper of natural law, who 'brings naturally independent, autonomous subjects into relation and connection by contract', simply as an 'anticipation of "civil society"'.[16] However, the *Contrat social* would simply return to the Robinsonades of the eighteenth century, a critique of which, indeed, begins the *Introduction* of 1857.

3. In *Capital* (I, Chap. 30), on the other hand, Marx openly employs a (moralistic) criticism of the rich in his analysis of the expropriation of the 'multitude of small producers' by the 'great manufactories', to be found in Rousseau's *Discours sur l'économie politique* which, quoted by Marx, runs as follows: 'I shall allow you, *says the capitalist*, the honour of serving me, provided you give me the little you have left for the trouble I take to give you orders.'[17] However, it is also true that this quotation-tribute by Marx is far indeed from doing justice to the deep democratic (egalitarian) inspiration which, as we know, he received from Rousseau. For, thanks to the correction made by Marx replacing Rousseau's 'rich' – a term of generic sociological moralism – with the specifically materialist term 'capitalist', the quotation is clearly transformed into a new, socialist form. And compare the crucial substitution, in Marx–Engels's *German Ideology* of '*necessary* association', i.e. union 'on the basis of (*material*) conditions', in the place of 'by no means an *arbitrary* one, such as is expounded for example in the *Contrat Social*'.[18] However, regarding the *Contrat* one must at least observe that, even when its contractualist natural law theory is destroyed, its enormous influence on Marx himself has still to be explained. This influence is transmitted through its criteria of 'sovereign popular will', of the 'sovereign' which 'can be represented only by itself', etc. – as we have seen. The influence thereafter, too, bears on the whole historical development of socialism, from the Paris Commune of 1870 to the Soviet socialist state (with its 'democratic centrality').

4. In the cited *Critique of the Gotha Programme*, we find almost at the beginning that Rousseau is evoked as a kind of typical example of a semi-utopian, semi-rhetorical sociologist. Therefore, with the intention of scolding the inconsequentiality and superficiality of the Lassallean authors of the Gotha Programme, Marx writes as follows:

According to the first proposition [of the programme], labour was the source of all wealth and all culture; therefore no society is possible without labour. Now we learn, conversely, [in the second proposition] that no 'useful' labour is possible 'without' society. One could just as well have said that only in society can useless and even socially harmful labour become a branch of gainful occupation, that only in society can one live by being idle, etc. – *in short, one could just as well have copied the whole of Rousseau.*[19]

From this it is clear that this Rousseau who wrote the *Discours sur les sciences et les arts* and other comparable texts, Rousseau the rhetorical, *minor* critic of society, became for Marx, in the *literary* passion of his political polemic, neither more nor less than the *whole* Rousseau. (Cf. Rousseau's 'This is how luxury, dissoluteness and slavery have been for the whole of time the bane of the pretentious efforts we have made to escape from the happy ignorance in which eternal wisdom had placed us.')[20] Naturally, Marx's oversight is the more singular and remarkable because it occurs in that work of his most imprinted with the philosophical spirit of Rousseau the *major* critic of societies and of their inequalities and injustices, as seen above. This is at once a profound and unconscious contradiction.

No less contradictory and embarrassing than Marx's is the attitude of Engels towards Rousseau, though it emerges as more interesting and significant because of the historical sense of the complex problem of egalitarianism shown by Engels.

The relevant texts by Engels can be arranged as follows:

1. The judgements on the *Contrat social* which, sometimes, do strict justice to that theoretical masterpiece of modern democracy, as when Engels says that 'the *Contrat social* of Rousseau came into being, and only could come into being, as a democratic bourgeois republic' (*Socialism: Scientific and Utopian*, 1, 1877,[21] and *Anti-Dühring*, Introduction, 1878), or that Rousseau 'with his republican *Contrat social* indirectly overcomes the constitutional Montesquieu' (letter to Mehring, 14 July 1893).[22] And

sometimes, on the other hand, the judgements are below the level of truth and justice, as when Engels, for example, includes the *Contrat* indiscriminately in his condemnation of the abstract 'state based upon reason' and concludes in the manner of Hegel that the *Contrat* 'had found its realisation in the Reign of Terror'[23] (*Socialism . . . etc.*, 1).

2. The general judgement on the egalitarian idea is one which is formally, theoretically, correct to the following extent: he postulates that 'since the French bourgeoisie, from the great revolution on, brought civil equality to the forefront, the French proletariat has answered blow for blow [the "*proletarische Konsequenzzieherei*"] with the demand for social, economic equality'. He ends by saying that 'the real content of the proletarian demand for equality is the demand for the *abolition of classes*',[24] and that 'Any demand for equality which goes beyond that, of necessity passes into absurdity'[25] (*Anti-Dühring*, I, 10). (Cf. the *Vorarbeiten* of the *Anti-Dühring*: 'The equality of the bourgeoisie (abolition of class *privileges*) is very different from that of the proletariat (abolition of the classes themselves)'.[26] Yet this is a judgement which, if it is combined with the significance attributed by Engels himself to the influence of Rousseauan thought in the egalitarian movement, is shown to be lacking and defective in its historical reflections, since all that Engels *tells* us about the egalitarian Rousseau is the generic phrase that the idea of equality has 'especially thanks to Rousseau played a theoretical . . . role'[27] (*Anti-Dühring*). This is said despite the frank Rousseauan accents, those of the *greater* egalitarian-anti-levelling Rousseau, which we find in the critique by Engels of Dühring's abstract egalitarianism. There, for example, 'what interests us is [Dühring's] admission that, as a result of the moral equality between men, equality has vanished once more' (ibid.).[28]

If it is true that in the *Vorarbeiten* cited here (but only in them) there is an attempt to clarify that the 'bourgeois side' of egalitarianism was formulated in a manner '*on behalf of all humanity*'[29] by Rousseau, it is equally true that Engels immediately adds that 'As was the case with all demands of the bourgeoisie, so here too the proletariat cast a fateful shadow beside it and drew its *own conclusions (Babeuf)*.'[30] This is the same as saying that the only, or chief, conclusions drawn by the revolutionary proletariat from Rousseau's egalitarianism must have been the egalitarian, levelling and utopian corollaries of a Babeuf, that bad caricature of a hack (cf. for example the 'equal and honest mediocrity' of Babeuf beside the *Contrat social*, II, 11). All these are things which can explain but not justify the final judgement of the *Vorarbeiten* (and left there), that the principle of equality (defined here as 'there must be no privileges') is 'essentially *negative*' and that 'Because of its lack of positive content and its off-hand rejection of the entire past it is just as suitable for proclamation by a great revolution, 1789–96, as for the later blockheads engaged in manufacturing systems.'[31]

3. The specific judgement of the *Discours* on inequality, a judgement apparently very comprehensive and generous, is based on an attempted historical-dialectical analysis of some basic elements of the *Discours*. For example, 'For the poet it is gold and silver, but for the philosopher iron and corn, which have civilized man [human *individuals*] and ruined the human race',[32] and which concludes as follows:

Each new advance of civilization is at the same time a new advance of inequality [*among* men, or civil, political: cf. above, para. 1]. [. . .] And so inequality once more changes into equality; not, however, into the former natural equality of speechless primitive men, but into the higher equality of the social contract. The oppressors are oppressed. It is the negation of the negation [see Hegel]. Already in Rousseau, therefore, we find not only a line of thought which corresponds exactly to the one developed in Marx's *Capital* [*sic*], but also point by point a whole series of the same dialectical turns of speech as Marx used: processes which in their nature are antagonistic, contain a contradiction; transformation of one extreme into its opposite; and finally, as the kernel of the whole thing, the negation of the negation (*Anti-Dühring*, I, 13: cf. *Socialism*, etc., 1).[33]

Here it can be seen that Engels's tendency to search everywhere, indiscriminately, for precedents for the dialectic of historical materialism on the one hand concedes *too much* to Rousseau by placing him alongside Marx as regards historical method, but on the other hand he concedes *too little*. In this case, Rousseau's original research into equality is passed over – that of the reconciliation of the two types of inequality (of which only one, that of civil or political inequality is here taken up by Engels), and thus his specific (anti-levelling) egalitarianism is dissolved into a game of antitheses and syntheses – of inequality and equality – both generic and schematic, revealing the heavy Hegelian residue in Engels' conception of the dialectic of historical materialism. Hence, finally, this judgement of the *Discours* by Engels is re-attached, by its historical deficiency, to his general judgement of the egalitarian idea, reproduced above.

It seems to me that this is sufficient evidence of the confused knowledge the founders of scientific socialism had of their historical debt to Rousseau. (That this confused knowledge can be perpetuated in Soviet socialist culture is shown, for example in the *Introduction* by Vyshinsky, to the *Law of the Soviet State* (New York: Macmillan, 1948), where in a four-line footnote, compared with more than a page devoted to Kant-Kelsen, one finds the following: 'J.-J. Rousseau [. . .] an ideologist of the radical petty bourgeoisie. His famous *Du contrat social*, wherein his views as to public law are developed, exerted an enormous influence on the development of the bourgeois liberal-democratic theory of the state as the incarnation of the general will.'[34] For the rectification of the grave historical error which restricts the influence of the criterion of 'general will' and its implicit 'popular sovereignty' to the bourgeois state, see our remarks on *national*-popular, *bourgeois* sovereignty above – *Clarifications*, 5, 4 and 5, and also the note at the end of II, 7, for documentation of those elements of Rousseauan *direct democracy*, present in the Soviet constitution of 1936.

This historical debt, finally, can be expressed as follows: that the Rousseauan theorems of anti-levelling egalitarianism, mediating of persons, should be numbered among the essential historical and intellectual premisses of the concept-model of abolition of classes in a society of free (because equal) persons, such as the communist society set out hypothetically in the *Critique of the Gotha Programme*, in *Anti-Dühring*, and in *State and Revolution*. In this concept-model is expressed, therefore, together with the perfect 'proletarian [egalitarian] answer blow by blow,'[35] of which Engels spoke, that *positive* (Rousseauan) content of the egalitarian principle, which Engels disputed in the *Vorarbeiten* of *Anti-Dühring*.

NOTES

1. Cf. in addition the *Critique of the Gotha Programme*, I: 'This *equal* right is an unequal one for equal labour [. . .] Right by its very nature can consist only in the application of an equal standard; but *unequal individuals (and they would not be different individuals if they were not unequal)* are measurable only by an equal standard in so far as they are brought under an equal point of view, are taken from one *definite* side only, for instance, in the present case, are regarded *only as workers* and *nothing more* is seen in them, everything else being ignored' (*Selected Works*) vol. 2, op. cit., p. 24).
2. Lenin, *State and Revolution*, op. cit., pp. 465–6.
3. *Discours*, op. cit., pp. 131, 193–4.
4. *State and Revolution*, op. cit., p. 467.
5. ibid., p. 468.
6. *Anti-Dühring*, op. cit., p. 335.
7. *Discours*, op. cit., p. 189.
8. ibid., p. 223.
9. ibid., p. 222, note xix.
10. ibid., p. 207, note ix.
11. *La Nouvelle Héloïse*, op. cit., p. 612.
12. *Emile*, IV, op. cit., p. 614.
13. Marx, *Contribution*, op. cit., p. 28.
14. ibid., p. 85 (della Volpe has 'class society').
15. *On the Jewish Question*, op. cit., p. 167 (*Contrat social*, op. cit., p. 381).

16. Introduction of 1857, in *Grundrisse*, ed. M. Nicolaus (Harmondsworth: Penguin, 1973), p. 83.
17. *Capital*, 1, op. cit., Ch. 30, note 1, p. 746. Rousseau, *Œuvres*, 3 p. 273, op. cit.
18. *The German Ideology* (Collected Works, vol. 5 (London: Lawrence and Wishart, 1976)), p. 80 (della Volpe has 'voluntary' for 'arbitrary').
19. *Critique of the Gotha Programme*, op. cit., p. 19.
20. *Discours sur les sciences et les arts* (*Œuvres complètes* 3, op. cit.), p. 15.
21. In *Selected Works*, vol. 2, op. cit., p. 117.
22. ibid., p. 499.
23. *Socialism: Scientific and Utopian*, op. cit., in ibid., p. 119.
24. *Anti-Dühring*, op. cit., p. 128. Cf. Lenin, *State and Revolution*, V, 4: '*Democracy* means *equality*. The great significance of the proletarian struggle for equality and of equality as a slogan will be clear if we correctly interpret it as meaning the *suppression of classes*. But democracy means only *formal* equality. And as soon as equality is achieved for all members of society *in relation to ownership of the means of production*, that is, equality of labour and wages, humanity will inevitably be confronted with the question of advancing further, from formal equality to actual equality, i.e. to the operation of the rule: "from each according to his capacity, to each according to his needs"' (op. cit., p. 472). These conclusions by Lenin are important as regards the problematic of democracy and equality. Leninist reasoning should be explained and understood as follows. It is true that democracy means equality (social, in full), but as (social) equality means precisely the suppression of classes, *actual*, real (*social*) equality will come into being only with their suppression (and that of the state). That is, in communist society: 'from each according to his ability, to each according to his needs.' Consequently, this same socialist democracy (as a property of the socialist state) still entails a *formal* (social) equality, for it is indeed, a (complex) class phenomenon. For example, in the socialist state the unjust 'equal right' for 'unequal' subjects is still in force, that is, bourgeois right and, on the other hand, its state foundations lie in the mass of the proletariat.

Naturally, despite this, one detracts not at all from the enormous progress represented by socialist democracy – as regards equality – compared with that (inferior) type of *formal* equality. This is the *political* equality constitutive of parliamentary democracy, or rather of the liberalism specific to the bourgeois state. Hence the *other* Leninist criticism of democracy, for example in *The Proletarian Revolution and the Renegade Kautsky*, can be understood, when he says: 'Even in the most democratic bourgeois state the oppressed people at every step encounter the crying contradiction between the *formal* equality proclaimed by the "democracy" of the capitalists and the thousands of *real* limitations and subterfuges which turn the proletarians into *wage slaves*' (*Collected Works*, op. cit., vol. 28, p. 246). This means only that socialist democracy, i.e. the socialist state with its legality, does not yet realize the actual social equality produced by communist society, beyond class. It remains true, however, that, formal as it is, the equality produced by the socialist state marks enormous progress made over the past, in that it does indeed deal with social equality, and no longer simply with political equality (and thus the term 'formal' used in the two cases in Lenin's critique has an ideal-historical value very different in each case). For these problems, see above (end of II, 7, and *Clarifications*, 5, nos. 4 and 5), whose conclusions are confirmed and further clarified by the preceding. So, 'social democracy' and 'libertarian equality' are there contrasted as 'substantial' against 'political democracy' and 'civil liberty'. However, that does not preclude or contradict their *formal* character in relation to communist equality and freedom. Insofar as they too are class categories, they are destined to wither away in communist society, wither together with the socialist state, of whose legality they form *one* component.

25. *Anti-Dühring*, op. cit., p. 128.
26. ibid., p. 409.
27. ibid., p. 124.
28. ibid., p. 122.
29. ibid., p. 407.
30. ibid.
31. ibid.
32. ibid., p. 167.
33. ibid.
34. Vyshinsky, op. cit., note 44 to p. 169.
35. Adapted from *Anti-Dühring*, op. cit., p. 128.

4 WE AND THE CONSTITUTION

(*à propos* State of law and democracy)

I shall mention only three points. The *first* is this: of what significance, for a philosophico-political discussion, is the ill-reputed 'fraud law', against which in its day the deputies of the left fought?* We are dealing, of course, with the electoral law of 31 March 1953, no. 148, intended to limit – by technical subleties which we shall pass over – nothing less than the effective enforcement of the principle of universal suffrage. Mortati, a member of the Constitutional Court, writes in his *Institutions of public law*, '. . . effectively it seems that it [the law] conflicted with more than individual opinions, that is, with the informing spirit of the whole system which tends to ensure a correspondence between the distribution of political forces within parliament and that existing in the country.'[1]

Therefore, what can this mean (from the point of view of political philosophy) except that *Kantian* spirit of the 'state of law' once again aims at contesting and (*faute de mieux*) reducing universal suffrage, which is a typically *Rousseauan* principle and, if nothing more, a specifically democratic institution? Consequently, does the danger of ideological confusion not already become clear as regards those, like comrade Gerratana (in *Società*, 1961, 6),[2] who tend to overlook the specific difference between Kantian and Rousseauan political doctrine, and hence that between *parliamentary democracy*, or 'State of law', and *social democracy*, or democracy in the highest sense? Every principle (in this instance, political) has its strict, unavoidable logic, which obliges us to distinguish between these principles with extreme care, so as not to make subsequent errors in their choice and application.

* See the explanatory note in *Clarifications*, 4.

Second point: still speaking philosophically, what is the meaning of the first article of the constitution by which 'Italy is a democratic republic founded on labour', etc. Let us first hear the comment of a jurist like Mortati.

He advises us that this article means

on the one hand to challenge the pre-eminent position accorded in previous documents to other values (like private appropriation of the means of production) and, on the other, to assign to *labour* the function of *supreme evaluative criterion* of the *position to be attributed to citizens in the State*, as it was held to be the *most suitable* to express the *value of the person*, the *creative capacity* enclosed within him, and the better course to make him pay the debt contracted with society.

From this

the consideration of labour as the informative value of social ordering implies that the *comparative title* of the *social value* of the citizen should be deduced from his *capacities*, *not* just from social positions acquired *without merit* by the subject who enjoys them, and additionally it requires that each be given the possibility of taking on the working activity most congenial to his own aptitudes, drawing from it the means of satisfying the needs inherent in the human character (della Volpe's emphasis).[3]

Consequently: in comparison with, and against, Kant, who asserts that a labouring man has only 'a market price' and 'not [human] dignity', and consequently has 'no civil independence' and is deprived of the right to vote – (not for nothing is Kant the greatest theorist of that state of law with the 'freedom' of possession of the means of production as its basis, as above) – in comparison with and against Kant, we find Rousseau. Rousseau argues that in a 'well set-up' state 'the *ranks* of the citizens should be regulated [. . .] according to the real *services* [i.e. 'proportional to their talents and their strength'] which they give to the state'.[4] This is Rousseau as spokesman for the *personal merits of each*, and yet theorist of an egalitarianism which mediates between persons, anti-levelling *par excellence*.

Therefore, to continue, still bearing in mind how much separates the teachings of these two classics of modern political philosophy, it is possible to grasp the (complex) nature of that type of contemporary state which is embodied in the present Italian constitution. This is precisely because of the intermingling in the constitution of the differing and opposed influences of the doctrine of the state of law and that of the egalitarian state, democratic in the higher sense. Only in this way shall we do justice, apart from anything else, to the democratic-revolutionary spirit of the communist and socialist comrades who fought for this constitution in the Constituent Assembly.

Third (final) *point*: the need to determine rigorously the reasons and aim of our commitment to struggle for the application of the present constitution in the letter and the spirit. This supposes that there is a clear understanding not only and not so much of what that state of law means *as written down* but rather of what *this inclusion or insertion* of egalitarian or democratic-social aims means in the corpus of traditional, bourgeois, civil or political freedoms. For liberals and our opponents in general think it sufficient to exalt and defend the state of law (even additionally erasing the difference between Kant and Rousseau, reducing the second to the first, as Professor Giorgio Del Vecchio, for example, has already done), but we must ourselves think of defending whatever social democracy has been inserted in our constitution (even as a basically bourgeois one). We shall not succeed in this without clear ideas on what distinguishes parliamentary democracy from social democracy or, if you prefer, the liberalism of Kant and his followers from the democracy of Rousseau (and Marx and Lenin).

In other words, we must be aware of the fact that our constitution, as the lawyers say, is of a compromise type. It is so 'in the sense that it is held to be possible to combine private freedom and social interest, without, however, deriving this combination as liberal ideology did, from "preconstituted harmonies", but rather entrusting it to the

moderating interventions of the state' (Mortati). For the
state, he goes on, 'the crucial point is to decide the *quid
agendum* (what is to be done) when experience shows the
impossibility of reconciling the privatist regime of an
enterprise with social ends'. And: 'the predominance of
the latter over the former seems to be argued precisely by
basic principles and the subordinate position given by
them to hereditary rights', so that the same '*democratic
personalist* requirement', mentioned above, should be
satisfied 'at least' by 'assuring to all the primordial right,
superior to all others, of that to a job' (and see the 'right to
work' proclaimed by Article 4, whose subject, says Mortati,
is 'the adoption by the state of measures sufficient to create
full employment').

Here are outlined all those juridical features of a
democratic compromise which should be the objectives of our
present political battle, in order that they should not
simply remain on paper. These include the decree-law of
16 September 1947 on the so-called 'taxability of the
labour force', whose constitutionality is upheld by Mortati
as follows, against a contrary decision by the
Constitutional Court: that the decision 'could be made
insofar as (a) it has interpreted the last paragraph of Art.
41 contrary to its intention, in the sense, that is, that state
interventions in private enterprises cannot assume a
coercive character; (b) it has neglected to estimate the
scope of the obligation of social function which Art. 42
imposes on private property; (c) it has distorted the
meaning of the intention of the institution of equitable
social relations, for whose enforcement Art. 44 provides
limits to agrarian enterprises'. It proceeds, in the state
interventions permitted by Art. 43, to eliminate monopoly
situations, where the article quoted allows, for particular
laws (the principle of generality is therefore excepted), that
monopolistic enterprises be expropriated to transfer them
to public bodies or combines of workers or users, when
they have the characteristics of a major national interest',
which means that 'equal norms apply for enterprises

connected with sources of energy (e.g. oil) or to national public services' (Mortati). And so on.*

In conclusion, I have tried to show (very briefly) what and how many philosophical, or if you prefer principled, distinctions, are demanded and presupposed by a reply to an enquiry on 'the State of law and democracy'. All the more so if one considers the practical, immediate implication of such an enquiry, which is what conscious attitude to take towards our constitution, or its progressive aspects, as non-conservative democrats. This is one of those cases in which a philosophy of principles, so to speak, is rigorously required, as well as a moral duty, at least for a militant, democratic intellectual.

* Article 41 (extract): 'The law determines the appropriate programmes and controls in order that public and private economic activity may be directed and coordinated toward social ends.

Article 42. Property is public or private. Economic goods belong to the state, to organized groups, or to individuals.

Private property is recognized and guaranteed by law, which determines the methods of its acquisition and enjoyment and the limitations designed to assure its social functioning and render it accessible to all.

In cases prescribed by law, and on the basis of compensation, private property may be expropriated for reasons of general interest.

The law establishes the norms and limits of legitimate and testamentary succession and of the rights of the state in inheritance.

Article 43. For the purpose of general utility the law may originally reserve or may transfer, by means of transfer and war indemnity, to the state, to public bodies, or to communities of workers or of utilisers, specified enterprises or categories of enterprises which relate to essential public services or to sources of energy or to situations of monopoly and which have a character of preeminent general interest.

Article 44. For the purpose of securing a rational exploitation of the soil and of establishing just social relationships, the law imposes obligations and restrictions on private property in land: fixes limits to its extensions according to the region and agrarian zone: it promotes and requires reclamation, the transformation of latifundia, and the reconstitution of productive units: it aids the small and medium-scale proprietor.

The law frames provisions in favour of the mountainous zones.

NOTES

1. Costantino Mortati, *Istituzioni di diritto pubblico* (Padua: CEDAM, 1960, 5th edn).
2. Valentino Gerratana, 'Democrazia e stato di diritto', *Società*, xvii, no. 6, 1961.
3. Cf. the bibliographic note to *Clarifications*.
4. *Discours*, op. cit., p. 223 (della Volpe here translates 'ranks' as 'social positions').

FOR A MATERIALIST METHODOLOGY OF ECONOMICS AND OF THE MORAL DISCIPLINES IN GENERAL

(On Marx's methodological writings from 1843 to 1859)

1 THE POSTHUMOUSLY-PUBLISHED PHILOSOPHICAL WORKS OF 1843 AND 1844 (THE MATERIALIST CRITIQUE OF THE *A PRIORI*)

The first properly philosophical, methodological, works of Karl Marx are the two published posthumously, so-called juvenilia, which in the *Marx/Engels Gesamtausgabe* (MEGA)* are entitled: *The Critique of Hegel's Philosophy of Law* and *The Economic and Philosophic Manuscripts of 1844*, titles determined by the Russian editors, and in the latter case based on indirect allusions by Marx himself. For the first, one can speculate that 1843 was the latest date of composition (the subtitle is *Kritik des Hegelschen Staatsrechts* or literally *The critique of Hegelian state*, or *public, law.*) We, however, shall use the full title *The Critique of the Hegelian Philosophy of Public Law*, already used in our translation for Editori Riuniti, 1950.[1] For the second, the *Ökonomisch-philosophische Manuskripte aus dem Jahre 1844*, the date 1844 is determined by the title itself, and we know definitely the place of composition, Paris. On the other hand, Kreuznach was probably the place where the *Critique* was composed, presumably after the end of Marx's collaboration with the *Rheinische Zeitung*, which the 'Debates on freedom of the press'. 'The Law on Thefts of Wood,' etc., may recall.[2]

The most important of the two works in our view is the *Critique of Hegel's Philosophy of Law*,[3] even if till now it is incomparably less well-known in Italy and elsewhere than the *1844 Manuscripts*, despite the attention drawn to it by Marx in 1873, where, in the *Postscript* to the second edition

* The reference is to the edition edited by David Riazanov, Frankfurt, 1927 ff.

of Capital, he states literally: 'The mystifying side [*die mystifizierende Seite*] of Hegelian dialectic I criticized nearly thirty years ago, at a time when it was still the fashion.'[4] Subtract thirty from 1873 and you have the exact date, 1843.

This is the most important text since it contains the most general premises of a *new* philosophical *method*, in the form of that critique of Hegelian logic (through the critique of ethico-juridical Hegelian philosophy) with which Marx unmasks the 'mystifications' of the *a priori*, idealist, and generally speculative, dialectic. These are Hegel's *fundamental* logical contradictions, or substantial (nor merely formal) tautologies, which follow from the *generic* (*a priori*) character of the conceptual constructs of this dialectic. At the same time, Marx sets up against them that revolutionary 'scientific dialectic' to which he will specifically appeal in the *Poverty of Philosophy* (1847) and apply in *Capital*, after having specifically examined it for its relevance to economic problems in the *Introduction* of 1857 and the *Contribution to the Critique of Political Economy* (1859). The *1844 Manuscripts*, on the other hand, are of philosophical interest only in the last part, dedicated to the critique of Hegelian philosophy, which in any case can only be understood together with the *Contribution to the Critique of Hegel's Philosophy of Law*. For the rest they are economic-philosophic 'jottings', in places rich in brilliant insights into arguments and theories developed only later.

A cursory, but perhaps adequate, idea of the *Contribution*'s process of thought can be given by the following analysis of the Hegelian deduction of the passage from family and civil society to the state (paras. 262–9 of the *Philosophy of Law*, 1820).

Family and civil society [Marx says] are conceived [by Hegel] as *spheres of the concept* of the state, namely, as the spheres of its *finite* phase, as *its finiteness*. It is the state which *divides* itself into them [. . .] and it *does* this 'so as to emerge from their ideality as *explicitly infinite* actual *mind*'. . . . '*accordingly** [emphasis here

marked with an asterisk in a quotation from Hegel is always by
Marx] assigns to these spheres the material of its actuality *in such
a way** that this assignment, etc., *appears** mediated'. [. . .] At
this point the logical, pantheistic mysticism [of Hegel] becomes
very clear. The *actual* relation is this: 'with regard to the
individual the assignment of the material of the state is mediated
by circumstances, caprice, and the individual's own choice of
vocation' [by which a family is created, and one enters one of the
'estates' of civil society]. Speculative philosophy expresses this
fact, this *actual relation* as *appearance*, as *phenomenon*. These
circumstances, this caprice, this choice of vocation, this *actual
mediation* – these are [for Hegel] merely the *appearance of a
mediation* which the actual idea effects with itself, and which
goes on behind the scenes [in the 'mystery' of 'speculation'].
Reality is expressed not as it is [for what it is], but as another
reality. Ordinary empirical fact [the institution of the family,
real, historical, civil society] has not its own but an alien spirit
for its law; whereas the form of existence of the actual idea is not
an actuality evolved from itself, but ordinary empirical fact.

The idea [the predicate] is made the subject [substantified or
hypostasized] and the *actual* relation of family and civil society to
the state [or ideal] is conceived as its *internal imaginary* activity.
Family and civil society are the premisses of the state; they are the
genuinely active elements [since, as 'real subjects', Marx says,
they are 'real beings'], but in speculative philosophy things are
inverted. When the idea [the predicate] is made the subject [of
judgement], however, the real subjects, namely civil society,
family, 'circumstances', 'caprice', etc. become unreal objective
elements of the idea with a changed significance [they become
unreal predicates, meaning something else – 'allegories' of the
idea].

The assignment of the material of the state 'with regard to the
individual . . . mediated by circumstances [. . .]' is not expressly
stated to be what is true, necessary and absolutely warranted.
These (circumstances, caprice, etc.) are *as such* not presented as
rational. And yet, on the other hand, they are so presented
simply by being presented as a *seeming* mediation [or, cf. above,
as 'phenomenon' or 'manifestation' of the idea], by being left as
they are but at the same time acquiring the significance of being
an attribute of the idea, a result, a product [or property] of the
idea [. . .] There is a double history, an esoteric and an exoteric.

The content lies in the exoteric part [ordinary empirical fact]. The interest of the esoteric part [mystery of speculation] is always that of finding again in the state the history of the logical [or pure] concept. It is on the exoteric side, however, that development proper takes place [or there is at least a content!] [. . .]. (T)here can be no political state without the natural base of the family and the artificial basis of civil society; they are for it a *conditio sine qua non*. But the condition is postulated [by Hegel] as the conditioned, the determinant as the determined, the producing factor as the product of its product [the state]. The actual idea only degrades itself into the 'finiteness' of the family and civil society so as by transcending them to enjoy and bring forth its infinity. '*Accordingly*' (in order to achieve its purpose) it 'assigns to these spheres the material of this, its finite actuality' (this? which? these spheres are indeed its 'finite actuality', its 'material'). [. . .] Empirically reality is thus accepted as it is. It is also expressed as rational, but it is not rational on account of its own reason, but because the empirical fact in its empirical existence has a different existence from it itself [it is an 'allegory'!]. The fact which is taken as a point of departure is not conceived of as such [by Hegel], but as a mystical result. The actual becomes a phenomenon [of the idea], but the idea has no other content than this phenomenon. [. . .] The entire mystery [. . .] of Hegel's philosophy as a whole is set out in this paragraph [262]. [. . .] The transition of the family and civil society into the political state is, therefore, this [see para. 266]: the mind of these spheres, which is *implicitly* the mind of the state, now also behaves to itself as such and is *actual* for itself as their inner core. The transition is thus derived, [in Hegel's understanding] not from the *particular* [or specific] nature of the family, etc., and from the particular [specific] nature of the state, but from the *general* [preconceived or *a priori*] relationship of *necessity* to *freedom*. It is exactly the same transition as is effected in logic from the sphere of essence to the sphere of the concept. The same transition is made in the philosophy of nature from inorganic nature to life. It is always the same categories which provide the soul, now for this, now for that, sphere. It is only a matter [to Hegel] of spotting for the separate concrete attributes the corresponding abstract attributes [whence 'Speculative philosophy expresses this fact as the idea's deed'] [I.e. . . .] Hegel does not develop his thought with respect to the object, but develops the object according to a thought already existing in it [or pre-conceived, *a priori*].[5]

Compare now the remarkable, essential agreement with this final criticism of Hegel by Marx in the following critique by Galileo of 'Simplicio', who is really the Jesuit Scheiner, the scholastic astronomer: 'This fellow,' says Galileo in the words of Salviati, 'goes about thinking up, one by one, things that would be required to serve his purposes, instead of adjusting his purposes step by step to things as they are' (*Dialogue concerning the two chief world systems* . . . The First Day).[6]

A general critical conclusion: 'It is important,' says Marx, 'that Hegel everywhere makes the idea the subject [of judgement] and turns the proper, the actual subject [. . .] into a predicate. It is always on the side of the [mystified] predicate, however, that development takes place.'[7] That is, as seen above, it belongs to the 'esoteric part' or that of 'vulgar empirical fact', which really promotes development, or, better, where there is *nonetheless* a content. However, the vulgar empirical fact, as has also been shown, is left *as it is*, is *not* set forth, as such, as an empirical fact, as the *rational*, true and necessary, and hence is not analysed, but has only received from without, *a priori*, the value of a (generic) abstract attribute of the idea (or its allegory). The idea transcends it infinitely, and hence is of no use in truly casting light on it, or in mediating it. It remains, in short, as Marx says, 'badly empirical', an essential *tautology*, or tautology of *the fact* itself, the empirical fact *to be investigated*. From this results cognitive sterility, as a penalty and punishment for the *a priorization* or *allegorization* of the vulgar empirical. As Marx explains in his comment on para. 301, 'Hegel is not to be blamed for depicting the nature of the modern state [of his time] as it is, but for presenting that which is as the *nature of the state*.'[8] In other words, Marx means that by so doing, Hegel makes the historical state of that time *generic*, makes it the most universal *essence*, and yet puts himself in the position of being unable to see any longer what there was in its structure and (historical) origin that was particular or specific, and hence does not criticize it. Thus, one sees how Hegel's well-known exaltation, or *idealization*, of the 'constitutional', semi-feudal, Prussian monarchy of 1820 could occur.

Marx positively contrasts in the following terms his own philosophico-historical method with Hegel's philosophico-speculative or dialectical-*a priori*, thoroughly deficient, method. 'So the truly philosophical criticism of the present state constitution', Marx says in his comment on para. 305, 'not only shows up contradictions as existing; it *explains* them, it comprehends their genesis, their [historical] necessity. It considers them in their *specific* [historical] significance. But *comprehending* does not consist, as Hegel imagines, in recognising the features of the logical concept everywhere, but in grasping the *specific* logic of the *specific* subject'[9] (the last two emphases mine).

Thus it is already clear how the knowledge of that new dialectical materialist *method* comes into being here. That method, as dialectical-experimental (Galilean), comes to be applied to the (historico-dialectical) investigation in *Capital*, after a first taste of it in the *Contribution to the Critique of Political Economy*, whose rigorously methodological *Introduction* is decisively important for the structure of *Capital* itself, but would be very obscure but for the epistemological key provided by this so-called immature work. (However, the *Treatise on Human Nature* by David Hume, like Marx's the work of a twenty-four-year-old, is also one of the masterpieces of modern philosophy.) Epistemological categories like 'determinate abstraction' and the fundamental 'tautology', which articulate the *Introduction*, would not in fact be clear without the precedent set up by the 'specific conception' just encountered, and by the whole critique indicated here of 'pure concepts' or 'generic' concepts of which the Hegelian dialectic is made up, as being precisely a 'mystified' dialectic, or 'counterfeit' in the eyes of Marx, young indeed but already so distant from the Master.

As for the general critique of the dialectic of pure concepts, the originality of this new, really materialist, kind of critique of all *a priori*, lies in its discovery of the effective consequence of any *a priori* abstraction, generic or hypostatic. This is not just the 'emptiness' of these abstractions (as in the anti-rationalist, Kantian mould, shared also by Feuerbach), but rather their *(faulty) fullness*, a fullness of un-mediated, or *un-digested, empirical contents*, in fact, which in turn are *transcended* by these *generic* (preconceived or *a priori*) abstractions. This is a faulty fullness, and thus a negative one from the cognitive (and epistemological) point of view, as it involves, we have seen, the presence of circularities or tautologies *of facts*, and hence, *in fact*, basic tautologies, not merely formal or verbal ones.

One type of criticism which nonetheless re-associates itself and aligns itself with the most profoundly anti-dogmatic criticisms known in the history of human thought, and which develops them, is the Aristotelian critique of the *a priori* Platonic classification of empirical species, and the Galilean critique of just that '*a priori* argument' of the scholastic physicists of his time. (We cannot spend time on this here and must refer the reader to our *Logic as positive science* and to the *Summary outline of a method* in this volume).*

This is a thoroughly *materialist* type of criticism, we argue, since that faulty, negative circle it criticizes is revealed as the consequence of all *a priori* reasoning. This vicious circle is none other than the counterpart, and confirmation, of that correct, positive circle of matter and reason, and of all non-*a priori*, non-dogmatic, and scientific (-materialist) reasoning. This demonstrates, in fact, how *one should necessarily infer the positivity and indispensability of matter itself as epistemological moment*, or element of the act of cognition, *from the faultiness and sterility of all (a priori) reasoning which does not take into account matter or*

---

* Not included in this edition.

the extra-rational in general. (This is a kind of critical postulate or axiom of matter.)

As for the application of this general criticism of abstract dialectics to Hegel's *Philosophy of law*, it is enough here to recall the following results: 1. the devastating criticism of what Marx calls the 'sanctioned lie' of the 'modern representative state', or the concept of a *'popular-class* representation'. This, says Marx, is a political illusion and a lie, as the class, the part, cannot represent the whole, the 'people', the 'general concern' or state interest. From this comes his sharpest analysis of the 'formalism' of bourgeois public law: as he says:

The constitutional state is the state in which the state interest as the actual interest of the nation exists *only* formally [. . .] (T)he state interest [. . .] has become a *formality*, the *haut goût* of national life, a *ceremonial*. The *estates* element is the *sanctioned, legal lie* of constitutional states, the lie that the *state* is the *nation's interest*, or that the *nation* is the *interest of the state*. This lie reveals itself in its *content* [i.e., the legislated, protected interests are only those of a class, the bourgeoisie!]. It has established itself as the *legislative* power ['the *form*'], precisely because the legislative power [emerging historically as the 'parliamentary' claim for 'natural' bourgeois liberties against absolute executive power] has [or should have!] the general for its content [. . .].[10]

But it does not have it, and its generality is hence merely formal, having long been too partial and exclusive of new social interests developed historically, without taking account of *a priori* 'natural' rights! This criticism is contained in the comment to para. 301 of Hegel's *Philosophy of Law*, where he says: 'The element *of the estates* [or classes] has the attribute which brings into existence the *general concern* not only *in itself* but also *for itself*', etc.

2. This specific critical examination of the bourgeois, Hegelian conception of the 'general concern', like the specific examination of the continual contamination in Hegel of Haller's* *legitimism* with Montesquieu's

* Karl Ludwig von Haller (1768–1854), Swiss lawyer and historian, a supporter of absolutism.

constitutionalism, and so on, are only a display of examples of that 'vulgar empiricism', empiricism (or history) which is *un-digested*. Empiricism, that is, *not* mediated or explained and hence faulty, *tautological*, which, we see, is the result and punishment of the abstract, Hegelian dialectic, and of any *a priori*. From this can be derived confirmation of the validity of the general materialist criticism of the *a priori*, and thus the manifest need to replace any philosophico-speculative conception by one which is philosophico-historical, or sociologico-materialist. In particular, one should think of the continuation into our own times, by way of Binder* and Gentile, for example – the latter author of a fascistic theory of the 'ethical state' – of the misleading influence of the *Philosophy of Law*, already silently taken apart by the criticism of the young Marx.

To finish up with the three *Economic and Philosophic Manuscripts of 1844*, given what has been already set forth above, it is enough to draw attention to the following elements. First, the most noteworthy concept of the philosophy of economics outlined there is the polemical-critical concept of labour as *estranged labour*.

We proceed [says Marx in the last section of the first manuscript], from an *actual* economic fact. [. . .] The worker becomes an ever cheaper commodity the more commodities he creates. The *devaluation* of the world of men is in direct proportion to the *increasing value* of the world of things. *Labour* produces not only commodities: it produces itself and the worker as a *commodity* . . . This fact expresses merely that the object which labour produces – labour's product – confronts it as *something alien*, as a *power independent* of the producer. [. . . Under these [bourgeois] economic conditions this realisation of labour appears as a *loss of realisation* for the workers objectification [labour fixed in an object] as *loss of the object and bondage to it*; appropriation as *estrangement*, as *alienation*. [. . Thus] the more objects the worker produces the less he can

* Julius Binder (1870–1939), German jurist and philosopher author of the neo-Hegelian *Philosophie des Rechts* (1925).

possess and the more he falls under the sway of his product, capital, etc.[11]

Second, there is a general methodological conception of the *unity* of human history and natural history, and hence of the *scientific* unity of knowledge – dialectical and moral Galileanism.

History itself [says Marx in the second section of the third manuscript], is a *real* part of *natural history* – of nature developing into man. Natural science will in time incorporate into itself the science of man, just as the science of man will incorporate into itself natural science: there will be *one* science.[12]

Hence, this means *unity* of *logic*, the philosophical, cultural revolution which is Marxism itself, as we shall see further on.

Third, we see the following characteristic of the Hegelian, idealistic method as the method which *allegorizes* the empirical (see above).

Real man [says Marx in the last section of the third manuscript] and real nature [i.e. that of 'real subjects'] become [for Hegel] mere predicates – *symbols* of this hidden, unreal man and of this unreal nature [the idea: i.e. they become predicates of the *substantified* idea, or predicates of their natural predicate – mystified predicates!]. Subject [or particular] and predicate [or general] are therefore related to each other in absolute reversal [*Verkehrung*] – a *mystical subject-object* or a *subjectivity* [i.e. generality] *reaching beyond the object* [or particular, or nature].[13] etc.

And he adds the happy description of 'uncritical positivism' to the 'vulgar' or faulty empiricism which is the result and punishment of the allegorization mentioned above. He adds too the no less happy synthetic formula of 'philosophical *dissolution* and *restoration* of the existing empirical world',[14] used to point to the whole mystifying process of the *a priori* or allegorical dialectic and its negative result.

However, in concluding we cannot pass over the biting

satire, artistic as well as philosophical, in these two posthumous publications, and how they foreshadow also in this respect the liveliest writings published afterwards. We must necessarily leave aside the philosophical irony directed against the Hegelian 'deduction' of the person of the prince, the monarch – it is enough to recall the phrase 'political zoology' which condemns the 'deduction' of the right of descent, the heredity of the prince.[15] We shall indicate just a few lines, from the *Contribution*, against the Restoration bureaucracy – but which naturally have a further relevance outside that period.

Marx says:

The bureaucratic spirit is a jesuitical, theological spirit through and through. The bureaucrats are the jesuits and the theologians of the state. The bureaucracy is *la république prêtre*. [. . .] It is therefore obliged to pass off the form for the content and the content for the form. State objectives are transformed into objectives of the department, and department objectives into objectives of the state. [. . .] The bureaucracy is the imaginary state alongside the real state – the spiritualism of the state. Each thing has therefore a double meaning, a real and a bureaucratic meaning [. . .].[16]

Against the speculative, Hegelian 'construction' of 'administrative science' and administrative 'examinations', Marx writes:

The *examination* – this 'link' between the 'office of state' and the 'individual', this objective bond between the knowledge of civil society and the knowledge of the state – is nothing but the *bureaucratic baptism of knowledge*, the official recognition of the *transubstantiation* of profane into sacred knowledge (in every examination, it goes without saying, the examiner knows all). One does not hear that the Greek or Roman statesmen passed examinations. But of course, what is a Roman statesman against a Prussian government official![17]

Against the Hegelian 'construction' of the 'moral and intellectual education' of the 'civil servant' he writes:

In the civil servant himself – and this is supposed to humanize him and make 'behaviour marked by dispassionateness, uprightness and kindness' 'customary' – 'direct moral and intellectual education' is supposed to provide the 'spiritual counterpoise' to the mechanical character of his [administrative] knowledge and of his 'actual work'. As if the 'mechanical character' of his 'bureaucratic' knowledge and of his 'actual work' did not provide the 'counterpoise' to his 'moral and intellectual education'! [. . .] The man within the official is supposed to secure the official against himself. But what unity! *Spiritual counterpoise.*[18]

And so forth.

As for the *Manuscripts*, it is sufficient to recall the following ironic note on two reactionary opponents of transferrable property and the 'miracle of industry':

See on the other hand the garrulous, old-Hegelian theologian Funke* who tells us, after Herr Leo,† with tears in his eyes how a slave had refused, when serfdom was abolished, to cease being the *property of the gentry*. See also the *patriotic visions of Justus Moser*,‡ which distinguish themselves by the fact that they never for a moment . . . abandon the respectable, petty-bourgeois 'home baked', ordinary, narrow horizon of the philistine, and which nevertheless remain *pure* fancy. This contradiction has given them such an appeal to the German heart.[19]

It is the patronizing smile of a Voltaire at the 'fourth estate' which here afflicts these last individuals infatuated by 'feudal souvenirs' (another expression from the *Manuscripts*)[20] – the last opponents of the revolution of the 'third estate'.

NOTES

1. Referred to hereafter as *Contribution to the Critique of Hegel's Philosophy of Law* (*Collected Works*, vol. 3, London: Lawrence and Wishart, 1975).

   * Georg Funke, a conservative Hegelian.

   † Heinrich Leo (1799–1878), author of a history of the Middle Ages (1830).

   ‡ Justus Moser (1720–94), Osnabrück lawyer, author of the *Patriotische Phantasien* (1774–6).

2. In *Collected Works*, vol. 1 (London: Lawrence and Wishart, 1975).
3. Note that the well known piece published in 1844 in Paris, in the *Annales franco-allemandes*, which the title, *Contribution to the Critique of Hegel's Philosophy of Law, Introduction* (Collected Works, vol. 3) has only an indirect connection with the *Contribution*, and so remains outside our present concern.
4. 1873 Postface to *Capital*, 1.
5. *Contribution*, op. cit., pp. 7–10.
6. Galileo Galilei, *Dialogue Concerning the Two Chief World Systems – Ptolemaic and Copernican* (Berkeley: University of California Press, 1953), p. 94.
7. *Contribution*, op. cit., p. 11.
8. ibid., p. 63.
9. ibid., p. 91.
10. ibid., p. 65 (GdV translates estates as classes).
11. Marx, *Economic and Philosophic Manuscripts of 1844* (*Collected Works*, 3 (London: Lawrence and Wishart, 1975)), pp. 271–2.
12. ibid., pp. 303–4.
13. ibid., p. 342.
14. ibid., p. 332.
15. *Contribution*, op. cit., p. 106.
16. ibid., pp. 46–7.
17. ibid., p. 51.
18. ibid., p. 53.
19. *Economic and Philosophic Manuscripts*, op. cit., p. 287.
20. ibid.

2 THE *POVERTY OF PHILOSOPHY* (1847)

(The emergence of the problem of a scientific, analytical dialectic.)

The *Poverty of Philosophy* was written in French between December 1846 and June 1847, and published with the title: *Misère de la philosophie. Réponse à la philosophie de la misère de M. Proudhon par Karl Marx*, etc. The German translation of the *Poverty*, edited by Bernstein and Kautsy, appeared in Stuttgart in 1885, the second edition in 1892. The work of Proudhon's to which it 'replies' is the *Système des contradictions économiques ou Philosophie de la misère* (1846). The *Poverty* was written, as Engels tells us in the preface to the first German edition, 'at a time when Marx had cleared up for himself the basic features of his new historical and economic outlook'. The Proudhonian *Système*, Engels goes on, 'gave him the opportunity to develop these basic features in opposing them to the views of a man who, from then on, was to occupy the chief place among living French Socialists. From the time when the two of them in Paris had often spent whole nights in discussing economic questions, their paths had more and more diverged; Proudhon's book proved that there was already an unbridgeable gulf between them. To ignore it was at that time impossible, and so Marx by this answer of his put on record the irreparable rupture.'[1]

How is this famous reply by the founder of scientific socialism to the petty-bourgeois, utopian socialist, one of the founders of anarchism, set out? The *Poverty* is planned in two parts, the first directed against Proudhon the economist, the second against Proudhon as philosopher. This corresponds to what is already suggested in the *Foreword*, in the following biting terms:

In France, he [Proudhon] has the right to be a bad economist, because he is reputed to be one of the ablest of German [i.e. Hegelian] philosophers. In Germany, he has the right to be a bad philosopher, because he is reputed to be one of the ablest of French economists. Being both German [i.e. philosopher] *and* economist at the same time, we desire to protest against this double error.

The reader will understand that in this thankless task we have often had to abandon our criticism of M. Proudhon in order to criticise German philosophy, and at the same time to give some observations on political economy.[2]

Naturally our concern here is with the second part of the work, the philosophical critique of the bad Proudhonian method, and of political economy in general, what Marx calls in short the traditional, bourgeois, '*metaphysics* of political economy'. However, we must start from the following specific statements and observations taken from the first part, which will introduce us, by way of the precise reasons which inspired it – i.e. Proudhon's economic errors, his economic utopia – to the second part.

What then, [asks Marx], is this 'constituted value' that constitutes M. Proudhon's whole discovery in political economy?

Once utility is admitted, labour is the source of value. The measure of labour is time. The relative value of products is determined by the labour time necessarily expended· in their production. Price is the monetary expression of the relative value of a product. Finally, the *constituted value* of a product is purely and simply the value which is constituted by the labour time incorporated in it.[3]

But, Marx objects, this concept of the *constituted* value of a product arises from a grave confusion. He points out that Adam Smith took sometimes the necessary labour time for the production of a commodity, at others the value of labour, as measure of value.[4] Ricardo had exposed this mistake, showing clearly the difference between these two criteria of measurement and concluding that 'the relative value of any commodity is measured by the quantity of labour embodied in it'.[5] Now, 'M. Proudhon outdoes Adam Smith in error by identifying the two things which the latter had merely put in juxtaposition.'[6] Thus all the 'egalitarian' consequences which Proudhon deduces from Ricardo's doctrine 'are based on a fundamental error'.[7] The consequences were, essentially, the abolition of any 'income without labour' through 'interest-free' loans by a People's Bank to the worker in exchange for a 'reciprocity of exchanges' which would allow the worker to secure the product of his labour without having to share it with those who did not work, the capitalists, and hence be able to become a small proprietor as well. In short, the claim was to destroy the fundamental characteristic of bourgeois property, income without labour, profit, nonetheless without compromising bourgeois property itself.

The error is

that he confounds the value of commodities measured by the '*value of labour*'. If these two ways of measuring the value of commodities were equivalent, it could be said indifferently that the relative value of any commodity is measured by the quantity of labour embodied in it; or that it is measured by the quantity of labour it can buy; or again that it is measured by the quantity of labour which can acquire it. But this is far from being so. The value of labour can no more serve as a measure of value than the value of any other commodity. [. . .]

If a muid [18 hectolitres] of corn cost two days' labour instead of one, it would have twice its orginal value; but it would not set in operation [would not feed] double the quantity of labour, because it would contain no more nutritive matter than before. Thus the value of the corn, measured by the quantity of labour used to produce it, would have doubled; but measured either by the quantity of labour it can buy or by the quantity of labour with which it can be bought, it would be far from having doubled. [. . .]

Thus it is going against economic facts to determine the relative value of commodities by the value of labour. It is moving in a *vicious circle*, it is to determine relative value by a relative value which itself needs to be determined.[8]

Proudhon ends up in this vicious circle when he seeks 'to

find out the proper proportion in which workers should share their products [and still enter into the area of the above 'reciprocity of exchanges'], or, in other words, to determine the relative value of labour, . . . (by) seek(ing) a measure for the relative value of commodities!'[9]

The thoughtless conception, [Marx resumes in *Capital*], that the cost-price of a commodity constitutes its actual value, and that surplus value springs from selling the product above its value, so that commodities would be sold at their value if their selling-price were to equal the price of the consumed means of production plus wages, has been heralded to the world as a newly discovered secret of socialism by Proudhon, with his customary quasi-scientific chicanery. Indeed, this reduction of the value of commodities to their cost-price is the basis of his People's Bank![10]

In principle [Marx concludes towards the end of the first part of the *Poverty*], there is no exchange of products – but there is the exchange of the labour which cooperates in production. The mode of exchange of products depends upon the mode of exchange of the productive forces. In general, the form of exchange of products corresponds to the form of production. Change the latter, and the former will change in consequence. Thus in the history of society we see that the mode of exchanging products is regulated by the mode of producing them. Individual exchange corresponds also to a definite mode of production which itself corresponds to class antagonism. There is thus no individual exchange without the antagonism of classes.

But the [so-called] respectable conscience refuses to see this obvious fact. So long as one is a bourgeois, one cannot but see in this relation of antagonism a relation of harmony and *eternal justice*, which allows no one to gain at the expense of another.[11]

We also read in *Capital*, whose most general criteria, that of the determination of distribution by production, and of its social, historical character, are already anticipated in the passage from the *Poverty* just referred to:

Proudhon begins by *taking* his *ideal of justice*, of '*Justice éternelle*', from the *juridical relations* that correspond to the production of commodities [the relations of *private proprietors* etc.]: thereby, it may be noted, he proves, to the consolation of all good citizens, that the production of commodities is a form of production as everlasting as justice. Then he *turns round* and seeks to *reform* the *actual* production of commodities and the *actual* legal system corresponding thereto, *in accordance with this ideal*. What opinion should we have of a chemist, who, instead of studying the *actual* laws of the molecular changes in the composition and decomposition of matter, and on that foundation solving *definite* problems, claimed to regulate the composition and decomposition of matter by means of the *'eternal ideas'* of *naturalité* and *affinité*? Do we really know *any more* about usury when we say it contradicts *justice éternelle* . . . and other *vérités éternelles* than the fathers of the church did when they said it was incompatible with *gràce éternelle*, *foi éternelle*, and *la volonté éternelle de Dieu*?[12]

These pointed reminders of eternal, abstract ideas, and the generic ideals of justice lead us naturally to move on to the second part of the *Poverty of Philosophy* – to its criticism of the 'metaphysics' of political economy and thus of the *a priori*, abstract nature of its logical or methodical basis. For these eternal ideas and generic ideals, both substantified or *hypostasized* by Proudhon, with their ultimate result of cognitive sterility – acknowledged in the question, 'Do we really know any more . . . ?' – are reminders which re-echo inflections already known to us from the previous chapter in the part devoted to the *Critique of the Hegelian philosophy of public law*.

At the start of the second part, Marx cites a very explicit passage from Proudhon's *Système*, which runs: 'We are not giving a history according to the order in time, but according to the *sequence of ideas*. Economic *phases* or *categories* are in their *manifestation* sometimes contemporary, sometimes inverted. . . . Economic theories have none the less their *logical sequence* and their *serial relation in the understanding*: it is this order that we flatter outselves to have discovered.' At once, Marx pointed out, 'M. Proudhon most certainly wanted to frighten the French by flinging quasi-Hegelian phrases at them. So we have to deal with two men: firstly with M. Proudhon, then with Hegel.'[13]

Coming to the heart of the question, he continues:

Economists express the relation of bourgeois production, the division of labour, credit, money, etc., as fixed, immutable, eternal categories. M. Proudhon, who has these ready-made categories before him, wants to explain to us the act of formation of these categories, principles, laws, ideas, thoughts.

Economists explain how production takes place in the above-mentioned relations, but what they do *not* explain is *how* these relations themselves are produced, that is, the *historical* movement which gave them birth. M. Proudhon, taking these relations for *principles, categories, abstract thoughts*, has merely to put into order these thoughts [. . .] The economists' material is the active, energetic life of man; M. Proudhon's material is the *dogmas* of the economists. But the moment we cease to pursue the historical movement of production relations, of which the 'categories' are but the theoretical expression [the 'theories'], the moment we want to see in these categories *no more* than ideas, spontaneous thoughts, *independent* of real relations, [hence *a priori*], we are forced to attribute the *origin* of these thoughts to the movement of *pure reason*. How does pure, eternal, impersonal reason give rise to these thoughts? [. . .] If we had M. Proudhon's intrepidity in the matter of *Hegelianism* we should say: it is distinguished in itself from itself. What does this mean? Impersonal reason, having outside itself neither a base on which it can pose itself, nor an object to which it can oppose itself, nor a subject with which it can compose itself, is forced to turn *head over heels*, in posing itself, opposing itself, and composing itself . . . *thesis, antithesis* and *synthesis*. For those who do not know the Hegelian language we shall give the consecrating formula: *affirmation, negation* and *negation of the negation* [a typical dialectical-triadic formula, the same as the above, and which expresses the 'rational affirmation' as made up of 1. a first 'affirmation' or immediate 'posing' of reason as undifferentiated unity; 2, a 'negation' or mere intellectual 'analysis' of it, or 'opposing' reason to itself; 3, the 'negation of the negation' or 'transcendence' of the analysis in the 'synthesis'. Hence this is the 'self-consciousness' of reason, its 'return to itself' as undifferentiated 'concrete' unity, or in short a 'composition' of reason with itself, – note, through a single intrinsic, *a priori*, absolute quality.] [. . .]

Is it surprising that everything, in the final abstraction – for we have here an [indeterminate] abstraction, and *not an analysis* – presents itself as a logical category? [. . .] Just as by dint of [indeterminate, *a priori*] abstraction we have transformed everything into a logical category, so one has only to *make an abstraction* of every characteristic *distinctive* [or specific] of different movements to attain movement in its [most] abstract condition – a *purely formal* movement, the *purely logical* formula of movement. If one finds in logical categories the substance of all things, one imagines one has found in the logical formula of movement the *absolute method*, which *not only explains* all things, but *also implies* the movement of *things* [endowing the concept, of the idea, with substantial reality – that is, hypostasis].

It is of this absolute method that Hegel speaks in these terms: 'Method is the absolute, unique, supreme, infinite force, which no object can resist; it is the tendency of *reason* to find itself again, to *recognize* itself in *all things*' (Logic, Vol. 111). *All things* being reduced to a logical category, and *every movement*, every act of production, to *method*, it follows naturally that *every* aggregate of products and production, of objects and of movement, can be reduced to a form of *applied metaphysics*. What Hegel has done for religion, law, etc., M. Proudhon seeks to do for political economy' (emphasis mainly della Volpe's).[14]

Therefore, 'Apply this method to the categories of political economy, and you have the [pure] logic and *metaphysics* of political economy,' you have the economic categories in an order not that of their 'logical sequence' (see above), just as 'for Hegel, all that has happened and is still happening is only just what is happening *in his own mind*.' Hence 'There is no longer a history according to the order in time, there is only the sequence of ideas in the "understanding" ' or, better, in reason. True, 'Economic categories are only the theoretical expressions, the ["exact"] abstractions of the *social* relations of production.' But M. Proudhon, 'holding things upside down like a true [speculative] philosopher, sees in *actual* relations nothing but the *incarnation* of these *principles*, of these categories' [i.e. he gives these categories, or ideas, the power of real entities, substantifies or *hypostatizes* them. In Greek, hypostasis is precisely a synonym for *ousia*, concrete substance or individual being]. Proudhon the economist has understood that 'men make cloth, linen or silk materials in definite relations of production. But what he has not understood is that these definite social relations are closely bound up with productive forces.' He has not understood that 'In acquiring new productive forces, men change their mode of production; and in changing their mode of production, [. . .] they change all their social relations.' It is 'The same men who establish their social relations in conformity with their material productivity' who 'produce also principles, ideas and categories, in conformity with their social relations.' *Thus* 'these ideas, these categories, are as little eternal as the [social, historical] relations they express', for 'They *are historical and transitory products.*'[15]

But bourgeois economists, and with them Proudhon,

have a singular method of procedure. [. . .] The institutions of feudalism [for them] are artificial institutions, those of the bourgeoisie are *natural* institutions. [. . .] When the economists say that present-day relations – the relations of bourgeois production – are natural, they imply that these are the relations in which wealth is created and productive forces developed in conformity with the [rational] laws of nature. These relations therefore are themselves natural laws *independent of the influence of time*. They are eternal laws which must always govern society. Thus *there has been history, but there is no longer any*. There has been history, since there were the institutions of feudalism, and in these institutions of feudalism we find quite different relations of production from those of bourgeois society, which the economists try to pass off as natural and as such, eternal [. . .]. Ricardo, after postulating *bourgeois production* as necessary for determining *rent*, applies the conception of rent, nevertheless, to the landed property of *all* ages and all countries. This is an error common to all the economists, who represent the bourgeois relations of production as *eternal categories*.[16]

Marx had already observed in the letter to Annenkov, of
28 December 1846 which, together with the 24 January
1865 letter to Schweitzer, form a valuable appendix to the
Poverty:

Indeed he does what all good bourgeois do. They all tell you
that in principle, that is, considered as abstract ideas,
competition, monopoly, etc., are the only basis of life, but that
in practice they leave much to be desired. . . . They all want the
impossible, namely, the conditions of bourgeois existence
without the necessary consequences of those conditions. None
of them understands that the bourgeois form of production is
historical and transitory, just as the feudal form was [. . .]. M.
Proudhon is therefore necessarily *doctrinaire*.[17]

Marx clarifies this conclusion in the letter to Schweitzer
as follows:

Every economic relation has a good and a bad side; it is the one
point on which M. Proudhon does not give himself the lie. He
sees the good side expounded by the economists; the bad side he
sees denounced by the [utopian] Socialists. He borrows from the
economists the necessity of *eternal relations*; he borrows from the
Socialists the illusion of seeing in poverty *nothing* but *poverty*' (i.e.
the *ethical*, negative aspect, not its economic, scientific causes].
Hence Proudhon's book is nothing but the 'petty-bourgeois
code of socialism'.[18]

Then in the same letter he restates very well the message
of the *Poverty*, saying Proudhon showed there

how little he has penetrated into the secret of *scientific dialectics*
and how, on the contrary, he shares the illusions of 'speculative'
philosophy. That is, regarding the '*economic categories*', '*instead of
conceiving them as the theoretical expression of historical relations of
production, corresponding to a particular stage of development in
material production*, he transforms them by his twaddle into pre-
existing *eternal ideas*, and in this *roundabout way arrives once more* at
the standpoint of bourgeois economy'[19] ('*er auf diesem Umwege
wieder auf dem Standpunkt der bürgerlichen Ökonomie ankommt*'; our
emphasis mostly – the emphases from 'instead' to 'material
production' and 'eternal Ideas' are Marx's).

The final epistemological observation by Marx, is that Proudhon finds himself in the end at the starting point, the *immediate* bourgeois economic point of view, as a result of following the *circle* of his Hegelianism, or metaphysical, *a priori*, hence *generic*, concern. This observation sends us back to the following points, casting a significant light on them: (1) The specific importance raised above, by that 'vicious circle', noted in the *Poverty*, which, for example, forms the determining of the value of commodities from the value of labour, one relative value based on another relative value, which in its turn needs to be established. (2) The general importance of the *cognitive sterility* (do we know by this any more at all about usury, for example, than the fathers of the church did when they said it was incompatible with eternal grace etc.?), which *follows* the *reforming* of the *actual* law corresponding to the *actual* production of commodities to *conform* with an abstract *ideal* of justice. This *follows*, in short, from any process of *hypostatization*, here penetratingly connected with those *a priori* procedures *par excellence* – theological arguments (here, the lay theology of idealism). This generally important point is raised in *Capital*, loc. cit. (3) We recall the following critical conclusion of Lenin, in '*What the 'Friends of the People' are* . . .' (1894),[20] that the (*a priori*) arguments of the metaphysical bourgeois sociologists are at best only a 'symptom' of the ideas and social relations of 'their time', but that they do 'not make the "understanding" of "real" social relations "advance by one iota."''

The key to the 'mystery' of the general 'scientific dialectic' whose revolutionary demand gives life to the whole polemic in the methodological section of the *Poverty* and the *Introduction* of 1857, later to provide the positive structure of *Capital*, is pointed out to us as an observation already in logical-critical form. Think here of the impressive, anti-dogmatic significance of what we quoted above, presented as the model for questions of economics, justice, or 'morals' in general, of the method or *essence* of *method* of the natural *scientist*, the chemist. What opinion should we have of a chemist who, instead of studying the *actual* laws of the molecular changes in the composition and decomposition of matter, and on that foundation solving *definite* problems, claimed to regulate the composition and decomposition of matter by means of the *eternal* – hence *generic* – ideas of naturalness and affinity? This key is the *materialist-historical analysis* of the *'mystified'*, twisted *structure* of the *a priori*, *speculative dialectic*, and its *ultimate consequences* which are those *tautologies* or logical inversions *not* simply *verbal* (cf. the 'circle' recalled above), which are discussed at the beginning in the examination of the basic *Critique of the Hegelian Philosophy of Public Law*.

With that we must finally move on to the *Einleitung* or *Introduction* of 1857, with its fertile development of the logical-materialist analysis of the twisted structure discussed above, and the consequent normative principles of this rectified logical structure expressed as economic *laws* (in fact), and the reasoning involved in them. In other words, this means the revolutionary transition – in economics – from the 'speculative' or metaphysical dialectic, 'mystified' or mystifying, to the 'scientific', i.e. *analytic*, dialectic. In other words, it is a passage from hypostasis to hypothesis, from *a priori* assertions to experimental forecasts.

NOTES

1. Marx, *The Poverty of Philosophy* (London: Martin Lawrence, no date), p. 7.
2. ibid., in *Collected Works*, vol. 6 (London: Lawrence and Wishart, 1976), p. 109.
3. ibid., p. 120.
4. ibid., p. 127.
5. ibid.
6. ibid., p. 128.
7. ibid., p. 127.
8. ibid., pp. 127–8.
9. ibid., pp. 128–9.

10. Marx, *Capital*, vol. 3, I, 1 (Moscow: Foreign Languages Publishing House, 1962), p. 39 (*Werke* (Berlin: Dietz, 1964), p. 49).
11. *Poverty*, op. cit., pp. 143–4.
12. *Capital*, vol. 1, op. cit., pp. 84–5, note 2.
13. *Poverty*, op. cit., p. 162.
14. ibid., pp. 162–4.
15. ibid., pp. 165–6.
16. ibid., pp. 174 and 202.
17. Letter to P. V. Annenkov, 28 December 1846, in *Selected Correspondence* (Moscow: Foreign Languages Publishing House, no date), p. 48.
18. Letter to J. B. Schweitzer, 24 January 1865 in ibid., p. 189. Della Volpe adds, in a note on the causes of poverty, 'Observing these, they would also see,' the text goes on, 'the revolutionary, subversive aspect which will overthrow the old society' (ibid.).
19. ibid., p. 188.
20. Lenin, *What the 'Friends of the People' are and how they fight the Social-Democrats, Collected Works*, vol. I (Moscow: Foreign Languages Publishing House, 1960).

3 THE *INTRODUCTION* (1857) AND THE *PREFACE* (1859) TO *THE CRITIQUE OF POLITICAL ECONOMY*

(The movement towards the solution of the problem of an analytic dialectic)

The *Introduction* (1857) to the *Contribution to the Critique of Political Economy* (1859) was discovered by Karl Kautsky in 1902 in Marx's archives, in the so-called *Nachlass*, and published by him in the issues of *Neue Zeit* for the 7th, 14th and 21st March 1903. It was republished in 1907 (again by Kautsky in the second edition of the *Contribution*), and finally in 1939 by the Russian editors who have given us a critically edited text of the fragmented and difficult manuscript (see now: K. Marx, *Grundrisse der Kritik der politischen Oekonomie* (Berlin: Dietz, 1953). In the (1859) *Preface* to the *Contribution*, which we shall discuss later, Marx had referred, however, to a 'general introduction' 'drafted' by him and 'omitted' on the grounds that it can be 'confusing to anticipate results which still have to be substantiated', and that the reader who wishes to follow him 'will have to decide *to advance from the particular to the general*'.[1]

Let us at once notice that this generic *scientist's* scruple, that of proceeding from the particular to the general, from facts to ideas and not (one-sidedly) vice versa, was to be finally argued out, explained, and developed in the omitted *Introduction* in Chapter 3, devoted to the 'method of political economy'. This scruple has no importance in itself, with respect to this methodological chapter which specifically interests us, but rather as regards the other chapters of concrete research, devoted to 'production' –

chapters on the other hand not themselves without illuminating methodological insights. In short, the fact remains that the 1857 *Introduction* is a work that stands by itself, with its own authority, precisely in that Marx gives us there a 'brilliant sketch' – as the most recent editors put it – of the 'methodical principles' of the application of the materialist dialectic to political economy, as well as basic concepts of historical materialism. We already know from the above conclusions something of the meaning of the logico-materialist analysis of method, which is the subject of this essay. Now we have to follow this analysis through its most incisive points.

If, for example, says Marx halfway through the chapter, we take the economic category of *production*, in its general aspect, we must realise that its *general* or common character, revealed by comparative analysis, is *articulated* and complex, and is *diversified* in numerous specific instances. Some of these elements are common to all periods, others only to a few. Certain characteristics will be common to the most modern period as well as the most ancient – they are characteristics without which no production could be undertaken. But just as the more developed languages have laws and characteristics in common with those less developed, and it is precisely the departure from the common, or general, which constitutes their 'development', so 'general' characteristics must be 'separated out' (*gesondert*) so that in the name of 'unity', uniformity, or generality, the 'essential' or specific 'difference' should not be forgotten.

Marx points out here how only a rigorous, scientific analysis of the general and the particular, and the 'separating out' of general characteristics, not confusing them with specifics, can avoid that 'forgetfulness' of the latter because of, or in favour of, the former. In short, only thus can one avoid the prevalence of the general over the specific which is the norm for the abstract synthesis of the *a priori*, the norm of *hypostases*.

The supposed 'profundity' of economists lies in this

forgetting, when they set out to prove the 'eternity and harmoniousness of the existing social relations.' They explain that *no* production is possible without an *instrument of production,* 'even if this instrument is only the hand', or, even if without past, stored-up labour, 'it is only the facility gathered together and concentrated in the hand of the savage by repeated practice'.[2] And they explain capital as a 'general, eternal, natural relation'. This is true *if* we leave out the 'specific character' which makes stored-up labour a 'capital' in the *modern* sense.

They tend, in short, to 'confuse and eliminate all *historical* differences', the *specific* ones, when they formulate their 'general human laws'. Thus (cf. John Stuart Mill, for example) they 'present *production* [. . .] as encased in eternal natural laws independent of history, at which opportunity bourgeois relations [of production] are then quietly *smuggled in* [*ganz unter der Hand . . . untergeschoben*] as the *inviolable* natural laws on which society *in the abstract',* in *general,* 'is founded'.[3] So, they fall continually into 'tautologies'. 'All production is appropriation of nature on the part of an individual within and through a *specific* form of *society.* In this sense it is a tautology to say that property (appropriation) is a precondition of production [appropriation]. But it is altogether ridiculous to *leap* [*Sprung*] from that to a *specific* form of property, e.g. private [modern, bourgeois] property.'[4]

Marx here wishes to tell us: (1), that the conclusion is ridiculous, since it is useless to define the determinate, specific, historical form of property, bourgeois property, by saying that as property, appropriation, it is a precondition of production or appropriation. This falls into a real tautology, or logical inversion. (2), that this tautological, and hence, from a cognitive point of view, *sterile* conclusion is none other than the result and *punishment* of a *hypostasis.* Precisely by having endowed the most *generic* concept of production as appropriation of nature with a powerful presence in *reality,* through the *a priori* method, it thus assumes and consumes within itself modern, bourgeois production *as well, so transcending* its *specific* characteristics. It has, in short, as Marx says, *smuggled in*, or replaced the specific meaning of bourgeois relations of production with the generic and unchanging conception of production, preconceived thus as the natural, eternal law of economic society *in the abstract*.

Hence, *metaphysical smuggling*, or *a priori replacement*, in favour of the generic, or most abstract, against the specific or most concrete *in the definition of the latter*, indeed shows us clearly the wrong, twisted structure of those arguments about the 'metaphysics of political economy' (see the *Poverty of Philosophy*, as discussed in the previous section). This is the structure and method of a mystifying dialectic which, we know, by reducing the specific or concrete to a mere 'allegorical' or symbolic manifestation of the Idea (with a capital letter), or the generic, finishes with tautologies or logical inversions which are confirmation of a *fraudulent*, hence *undigested*, non-mediated specific, or concrete quality. This fraudulent presence indeed involves nonetheless a presence of the concrete, but note the critical postulate of matter in the first section, and later the discussion of the 'evaporation' of concrete representation in *a priori* definition.

It is therefore necessary, Marx continues, to follow a 'scientifically correct method'. That means above all *proceeding* to *abstractions* (without which there is neither thought nor knowledge of any kind) *starting from the* '*concrete*' (*das Konkrete*), from the 'real subject', in this case an historical '*determinate* society'. The *Robinsonades* with which even today bourgeois economists amuse themselves – Robbins for example – are thus for Marx only 'conceits',[5] inspired by natural law theory. That is, 'Production by an isolated individual outside society – a rare exception which may occur when a civilized person in whom the social forces are already dynamically present is cast by accident into the wilderness – is as much of an absurdity as is the development of language without individuals living together and talking to each other.'[6]

However, while the 'concrete' is the effective starting point of observation and understanding it appears, nonetheless, *in our thought* as a process of syntheses, as a 'result' and 'not as a point of departure'. The concrete is concrete because, in fact, it is 'the concentration of many determinations, hence *unity* of the *diverse*'.[7] If, in order to examine the whole social process of production, we start from population as its basis, without really bearing in mind the 'classes', i.e. the concrete, historical elements which compose it, like wage labour, capital, etc., and the corresponding implications, we start from 'a *chaotic* conception of the whole'.[8] We arrive, by a step-by-step analysis, at increasingly simple concepts. In this, we proceed from an 'imaginary' (*vorgestellten*) concrete to *abstractions* even *less complex* (*immer dünnere Abstrakta*), to *genericity* (*Allegemeinheiten*), in order to reach the most simple abstractions, such as the division of labour, money, value, etc. This is the method pursued by bourgeois political economy: 'Along the first path the full conception *was evaporated* [*verflüchtigt*] to yield an abstract [in the pejorative sense] determination [*zu abstrakter Bestimmung*].'[9]

This determination – be it noted – is *not* 'empty', as the Kantian criticism of abstract rationalism would have it. Rather, the definition is *full of a* '*chaotic*', confused, *undigested concrete*, or non-mediated '*bad* empiricism' (see the first section, and earlier in this one). As we know, this abstract definition, weakened by its own *a priori* element, is converted into a real *tautology* – or one *of the real* or its *content* (the *punishment* mentioned above). Hence the 'evaporation' of concrete representation does not refer for Marx to its being emptied as representation, but to the 'chaotic', 'imaginary', *undifferentiated* character of its *content*. That is, what *evaporates* in the abstract, *a priori* definition, is the *cognitive value* of representation, *not its content*. This presence, or rather permanence, of the content, the concrete, matter, in the concept, come what may and however distorted (that is, as fraudulent content, hence chaotic, undifferentiated, or vulgar, non-mediated empiricism) may be expressed, explained, as we know, by the positive circle of matter and reason revealed by the *materialist* critique of the *a priori* and the corresponding critical postulate of matter (cf. the first chapter).

However, Marx continues, when we reach the simplest abstractions, such as the division of labour, exchange value, etc., 'From there the journey would have to be *retraced* [*rückwärts*] until I had arrived at the population again,' and 'this time not as the chaotic conception of a whole, but as a rich totality [unity] of many determinations and relations'.[10] In other words, Marx means that if the totality is thus examined in terms of its *historical character*, we are in this way following the *correct method*, by which 'abstract definitions [no longer in the pejorative sense, not *a priori*, but now based on the continual 'return' to the *concrete* as such, or unity-diversity] lead towards a reproduction of the *concrete* by way of *thought*,'[11] (and we know that without definitions or abstractions there is no thought or knowledge of any kind). In this way, Hegel 'fell into the illusion of conceiving the real as the product of thought concentrating itself'.[12] Whereas 'the method of *rising* [*aufzusteigen*] from the *abstract to the concrete* is the only way in which thought appropriates the concrete [or real], reproduces it as a concept in the mind [*geistig*]', being the real, or concrete in fact, 'the subject, [specific] society' is the 'presupposition' from which we start and this 'must always be kept in mind'.[13]

Consequently, the correct method can be represented as a *circular* movement from the concrete or real to the abstract of ideal, and thence back to the former (cf. the positive circle of matter-reason, discussed above). In other words, correct method consists, with logical precision, in a continual, invariable *historical explanation of abstractions* or (in particular) economic *categories* – if their *truth*, as we have seen, is in *inverse relation* to the *simplification* or *generic* abstraction of their *content*. It is the correct method, as Marx writes, to the extent that 'the path of *abstract* thought, *rising* from the simple to the *combined*, [or specific, concrete] would correspond to the *real historical* process'.[14] One can see this clearly in the correct, scientific elaboration of the basic category of *labour*.

Labour, says Marx, seems 'a quite simple category', a general one, and as an idea in this sense, as *labour in general*, is very *ancient*. 'Nevertheless, when it is economically conceived in this simplicity, "labour" is as *modern* a category as are the relations which create this *simple* abstraction.'[15]

This actually means that this category is certainly an *abstraction*, but *historical, not a priori*. That is, it *summarizes* the economic, practical and theoretical 'progress' made after that 'commercial and manufacturing activity', in which the source of wealth was transferred from the thing, money, to subjective activity such as commercial or manufacturing labour, up to the 'Physiocratic system' which pointed to its source in 'agricultural labour'. Finally, it led up to Adam Smith who discovered it in 'simple labour' or 'labour in general'. From this we have not only the character of activity as creative of wealth, but also the general character of the object defined as wealth, or 'the product as such, but labour as past, objectified labour'.[16]

Now, 'it might seem that all that had been achieved thereby was to discover the abstract expression for the simplest and most ancient [economic] relation in which human beings – *in whatever society* – play the role of producers'. And 'this is correct in one respect. Not in another.' It is true that 'Indifference towards any specific kind of labour *presupposes* a *very developed* totality of real kinds of labour, of which no single one is any longer predominant.' Thus, 'the *most general* abstractions arise *only* in the midst of the *richest possible concrete development*, where one thing appears as common to *many*, to all. Then it ceases to be thinkable in a particular form alone.'

On the other hand:

this *abstraction* of *labour as such* is not merely the mental product of a concrete totality of labours. Indifference towards specific labours *corresponds* to a *form of society* in which individuals can with ease transfer from one labour to another, and where the specific kind is a matter of chance for them, hence of indifference. Not only the category labour, but labour in reality has here become the means of creating wealth in general, and has ceased to be organically linked with particular individuals in any specific form. Such a state of affairs is at its most *developed* in the most *modern* form of existence of *bourgeois society* – in the United States. Here, then, for the first time, the point of departure of modern economics, namely the abstraction of the category of 'labour', 'labour as such', labour pure and simple [*tout court*] becomes true in practice.[17]

The economist Sweezy says: 'It is important to realize that the reduction of all labour to a common denominator, so that units of labour can be compared with and substituted for one another, added and subtracted, and finally totalled up to form a social aggregate, is not an arbitrary abstraction [. . .]. It is rather, as Lukács correctly observes, an abstraction "which belongs to the essence of capitalism".' So, as Marx concludes,

the simplest abstraction, then, which modern economics places at the head of its discussions, and which expresses an immeasurably ancient relation valid in all forms of society [cf. the possible objection earlier, that ('it might seem that all that had been achieved thereby, etc.')] nevertheless achieves practical *truth* as an *abstraction* [*nur in dieser Abstraktion*] only as a category of the *most modern society*.' 'This example of "labour" shows strikingly how even the *most abstract categories*, despite *their validity* – precisely because of their abstractness – for all epochs, are nevertheless, in the *specific character* of this *abstraction* [*in der Bestimmtheit dieser Abstraktion*], themselves likewise a product of *historic relations*, and possess their *full validity only for* and *within* these relations.[18]

And now we shall see another example of a basic *abstract* or *historic determination*, or a 'reproduced' *unity of diversity* – called *capital*.

Naturally, this *historical explanation of the categories* or economic abstractions, which forms the *concrete-abstract-*

concrete circle, does not mean in fact that one should adopt them 'in the same sequence as that in which they were historically decisive.' This would be 'unfeasible' [*untubar*] and 'wrong' [*falsch*]. For 'their *sequence* is *determined* rather by their *relation to one another in bourgeois society*, which is *precisely the opposite* of that *which seems to be their natural order* or which corresponds to [chronological] historical development'.[19] Thus, '(t)he point is *not* the historical position of the economic relations in the *succession* of different forms of society. *Even less* is their sequence '*in the idea*' (*Proudhon*)' – and as Hegel meant still more profoundly (see previous chapter) – but '(r)ather their *order within* [*um ihre Gliederung innerhalb*] modern *bourgeois society*'.[20]

Now, what exactly is the meaning of the Marxist rejection not only and not so much of the 'sequence [of economic categories] in the idea' (a rejection incontestable now after all that has gone before, and especially after the *Poverty of Philosophy*), but also of their 'natural sequence', the historico-chronological kind? What does the subsequent reference to their 'organic connection' within 'modern bourgeois society' mean, i.e. the reference to the sequence and order determined *by* their reciprocal relations in modern society (this latter order which is, we repeat, 'precisely the opposite' of their natural order)? 'The *logical* method of Marx in his critique of political economy,' says the entry in the *Great Soviet Encyclopedia*, 'is none other than the *historical* method, *only freed from the historical forms* [really: chronological] and all *disturbing accidents* [i.e. irrationality]'.[21] We add that the *real* question is that of not *confusing Marx's* method with *Hegel's* (which indeed comes out too free of historical accidents, disturbing or otherwise, even though it is claimed to be the method of historical dialectics!). This is the problem of seeing *how* the *essential historicity* of the economic categories *may be reconciled* with the *non-chronological* nature of their order (or 'inverse' order). This problem is simply the resolving development of the question of the concrete-abstract-concrete circle, that of the method of *determinate* or *historical abstraction*, hence the *scientific* abstraction. Let us examine this.

A decisive direction is given us already by the arguments made above on the *historical* formation of the *most modern* and also *general* category of *labour*. Here one sees that only as secondary to the latest, modern-historical character of *labour pure and simple* do the other (former!) historical characteristics of labour acquire a meaning which is *no longer historically bounded* nor chronologically fixed. In short, in the conceptual *synthesis*, represented by the abstraction of labour pure and simple, the different historical characteristics of labour are exchanged into conceptual forms, and hence take on a unitary, general meaning, losing their restricted, particularist, merely analytical, historico-chronological meaning – *without*, on the other hand, losing their specificity or meaningful *analytical power*, derived from their historicity or historical *necessity*. These are not fanciful characteristics!

From this is derived a *synthesis* which is also an *analysis*. This is the so-called historical or determinate abstraction in which real historicity and the ideal (non-chronological order) are reconciled. Of course, we have still to investigate further the *subordination* of former historical characteristics to the last historical characteristic, which is the principle of the formation of the historical or determinate abstraction as *synthesis-analysis*. This subordination, let us say at once, does not, cannot, mean anything other than the inclusion of those former characteristics in a nexus or concept whose formation can only be inspired by the latest, or *present*, historical characteristic, by, that is, *its problematic*.

Marx says:

The so-called historical presentation of development is founded, as a rule, on the fact that the latest form regards the previous ones at steps leading up to itself, and, since it is only rarely and only under quite specific conditions able to *criticise itself* [*sich selbst zu kritisieren*] [. . .] it always conceives them one-sidedly. The Christian religion was able to be of assistance in reaching an *objective* [not one-sided] understanding of earlier mythologies only when its own *self-criticism* [*Selbstkritik*] had been acomplished to a certain degree, so to speak, δυνάμει (potentially) . . .

that is, to become a history of religions.

Likewise, bourgeois economics arrived at an *understanding* [i.e. at an objective understanding] of feudal, ancient, oriental economics only after the *self-criticism of bourgeois society* had begun. Insofar as the bourgeois economy did not mythologically identify itself altogether with the past [through those *a priori* projections of categories, whether into the past or the future, which characterize hypostases], its critique of the previous economies, notably of feudalism, with which it was engaged in direct struggle, resembled the critique which Christianity levelled against paganism, or also that of Protestantism against catholicism. [. . .]' Hence, modern 'bourgeois society' *'for science as well'* 'by no means begins at the point where one can speak of it *as such*' (the last two emphases are Marx's).[22]

Let us move on to the formation of another basic determinate, or historical, abstraction, *capital*, typically brought into being by the latest or *present* historical characteristic of capital. That is, the abstraction is brought about by the *problematic* of capital, emerging from the *self-criticism* of society and *bourgeois* economics. In the medieval economy, says Marx, capital, except for that in the shape of money, has, in its form as traditional productive instrument, a landed-proprietary character. However, 'In bourgeois society it is the opposite', where 'Agriculture more and more becomes merely a branch of industry and is entirely dominated *by* capital'. Dominated, that is, by the dominant element 'the *social*, historically created element', where, if 'Ground rent *cannot be understood without* capital . . . capital can *certainly be understood without ground rent*'. Therefore, this element, capital, 'must form the *starting-point as well as the finishing-point*, and must be *dealt with before* landed property' (and only 'After both have been examined in particular (should) their interrelation be examined.').[23]

Here one sees in fact *how* the *meaning of the relation* between former economic categories, those of the past, or 'historical' (medieval landed property and corresponding capital), and the subsequent categories of modern society (rent and corresponding capital), is determined by an *'inverse' order* from that of the *chronological* order of categories. In other words, the order is not: landed property – capital, but capital – landed property. Thus the *reverse* order, or ideal, or value order, of the categories, which forms the meaning of the relation between past and modern, is determined by the *modern* or *actual* historical necessity of understanding and resolving the problematic of the phenomenon of *rent*. This is the 'organic connection' of relations and economic categories 'within modern bourgeois society' discussed earlier. This procedure demands for this purpose that capital must be the 'starting-point and the finishing-point', and be investigated 'before' landed property, *reversing* the (empirical) chronological order.

This is the substance of the 1857 *Einleitung*. The text, if we are not mistaken, allows us the following conclusions, when expounded more deeply, and consistently with the methodological principles Marxism–Leninism has uncovered, in *Capital* above all: (1) That an *objective*, not one-sided, *understanding* of its historical *precedents*, and hence of its *resulting* problems (e.g. rent), may be achieved by economics only to the extent that it is capable of *self-criticism*, and also aware of the *problematic* nature of its *own* categories. This presupposes (a) that it has acquired an *historical consciousness* of the *given concrete* or subject, that is, of *modern* bourgeois *society*, *contemporary* society, a consciousness lacking in bourgeois political economy. We have seen in the *Poverty of Philosophy* that in the perspective of bourgeois economy 'there has been history, but there is no longer any',[24] regarding as 'natural' or 'eternal' the specific institutions of that economy. (b) that it therefore be found fròm the start rooted without *a priori* or dogmatism on the very terrain of the *concrete* or *experience*, like every *science* worthy of the name. It should properly be found on the terrain of historico-*material*, *social* demands – the opening, or first movement of the above-mentioned circle *from the concrete* to the abstract. (2) That, consequently, it should formulate *abstractions*, for an objective understanding of its problems. Their nature as *syntheses*, a synonym for abstraction, concept, or category, *should be inseparable* from that of *analysis*, in that one is concerned positively to evaluate their historical *precedents*, and bring out the conceptual *connection* with their *consequences* or present and problematic historical features, and resolve these.

However, this must be done in such a way that the *ideal* or reverse order which the concepts thus assume does not lead to the total loss of their specificity or meaningful analytic quality, along with their restricted, isolated, in short merely analytical or historico-chronological reference. For the former is their historical appositeness and necessity. Such specificity or analytical equality is essential, since without it a *progressive*, synthetic-dialectical orientation is not even possible. This last is characteristic of concepts, is composed of them, and imprints on them the reverse, ideal, or rational order, or in short their connection with their consequences.

By this procedure *abstractions*, *syntheses*, or *unities*, are indeed formed, but as *specific*, analytical, ones, or those of *diversity*. These are, in short, abstractions in which the historico-*rational* demand may be satisfied as a demand in turn as function of the historico-*material* imperative, from which we started out. This is delineated jointly by the first and second movement – from concrete to abstract and *vice versa* – of the above methodological circle. It is a delineation, therefore, of the reconcilability (in the determinate abstraction) of historicity and intellectuality, or rationality. (3) Finally, as the *normativeness* inherent in the objectivity or rationality of the determinate abstraction – not a categorical or absolute normativeness, but only a *hypothetical* one – it is precisely expressive of *historico-*rational demands, and also of rational-*functional* ones (reason as function of matter and also the other way round). Thus, this hypothetical-normativeness cannot be *verified*, or acquire truth-value and become law-reality, save in and through historical (not abstract!) *materiality*, that of *practical* economic and social *experience*.

This is again depicted by the methodical circle in its second and final movement of *return* from abstract to concrete, which *thus closes the circle*. This was rigorously expressed by Lenin in *Materialism and Empirio-criticism* in these words: that

inasmuch as the *criterion* of *practice*, i.e. the *course of development* of all capitalist countries in the last few decades, *proves* only the objective *truth* of Marx's whole social and economic theory in general, and not merely of one or other of its parts, formulations, etc., it is clear that to talk here of the 'dogmatism' of the Marxists is to make an unpardonable concession to bourgeois economics.[25]

A concession, that is, to a really dogmatic economics, in so far as it was speculative or contemplative. For the decisive category of *practice*, never forget the second *Thesis on Feuerbach* where the following appears:

The question whether *objective truth* can be attributed to human thinking is not a question of theory but is a practical question. Man must *prove* the *truth*, i.e. [. . .] the *this-worldliness* of his *thinking* in *practice*. The dispute over the reality or non-reality of *thinking which is isolated from practice* is a purely scholastic question.[26]

The foregoing conclusions show us schematically the significance of that *scientific*, i.e. *analytic*, *dialectics*, of economics and the *moral* disciplines in general, towards which Marx was working from the *Poverty of Philosophy*, and from the anti-*a priori* polemic of the *Critique of the Hegelian philosophy of public law*. This dialectic is one of determinate or historical abstractions, criticizing and dissolving from within the speculative dialectic, or dialectic of generic, indeterminate *a priori* abstractions, wrong, mystified, and inconclusive – since as we well know, it ends up in tautologies of fact.

Now, the methodological importance of the scientific dialectic (symbolized in the concrete-abstract-concrete circle, or circle of matter and reason, induction and deduction) is little short of revolutionary. It means that any *knowledge* worthy of the name is *science*, hence not mere knowledge or contemplation. It means there is only *one* science because there is *only one* method, *one* logic. The *materialist* logic of modern, experimental science, it is understood, has taken science away from that more or less mathematizing Platonism, which is the philosophical background of science theoretically expressed by every bourgeois scientist from Galileo to Einstein. Hence, though the *techniques* which formulate laws certainly differ, as experience and reality differ – from the law of physics to that of economics and of morality, – the *method*, the *logic*, whose symbol is the above-mentioned circle, does not change. (Even though, for example, mathematics enters as an essential constitutive element in the formal elaboration of the laws of physics in general, on the other hand it can only be employed as an auxiliary instrument in the elaboration of economic and social laws and so forth.)

We know already from Marx in the *Economic and Philosophic Manuscripts* that

History itself is a *real* part of *natural history* – of nature developing into men. Natural science will in time incorporate into itself the science of man, just as the science of man will incorporate into itself natural science [that is, it will adopt its experimental method and have an historico-practical method in the historico-dialectical sense].[27]

And as Zhdanov puts it in his famous *Speech* on the history of Western philosophy:

The unique character of the *development* of philosophy resides in the fact that from it, as the scientific knowledge of nature and science developed, the *positive sciences branched off* one after another. Consequently the domain of *philosophy* [or speculation] was continually *reduced on account of the development of the positive sciences* (I might add that the process has not ended even up to the present time). This *emancipation* of the natural and social sciences from the aegis of [speculative] philosophy constitutes a *progressive process*, for the natural and social sciences as well as *for philosophy itself.*[28]

This means, finally, that the very progress of human knowledge permits us to affirm the *unity* not only of scientific logic, but also the *scientific* unity of *logic*, and, in short, the *unity* of *logic*. Thus, it is no longer permissible to propose a 'philosophical' logic distinct from that of 'science'. Philosophy as *science of man*, to use the expression in the way Marx mentioned earlier, is no longer 'science' in the metaphorical, groundless, misleading sense in which it is used, for example, in formulas such as 'philosophy as science of the spirit'. These are only synonyms for 'metaphysics', 'speculation', etc. Rather, it is in this specific sense of *history-science* or *materialist science of history* in which we indeed find, in the 1857 *Einleitung*, the first appearance, in outline, of an *epistemological-scientific* foundation of economics as science.

This can well be described as the *moral Galileanism* specific to Marxism: that is, that the traditional 'moral sciences' are really, and without exception, sciences in the most strict sense. We speak of *Galileanism* intentionally, to make a distinction between historical materialism and its method, both as regards *idealism* and its hypostases, and also, no less important, *positivism* and its idolatry of 'facts' and related Baconian repugnance towards *hypotheses* and ideas. Our journey with Marx in the period 1843–57 has led us, in fact, from the critique of the *hypostases* of Hegelian speculative philosophy to positive theoretical knowledge of the *hypotheses* of *Capital proved* therein, or turned into economic and social *laws*, as Lenin had correctly seen in *Materialism and Empirio-criticism* (1908).

If in conclusion we turn briefly to the *Vorwort* or *Preface* (two years later than the *Einleitung* of 1857), its well known philosophical content regarding the structure-superstructure relation are significantly revealing after what has gone before – especially the methodological *Introduction* of 1857. Let us recall the basic feature of its content. Marx says in reference to his 'critical re-examination of the Hegelian philosophy of law':

My inquiry led me to the conclusion that neither legal relations nor political forms could be comprehended whether by themselves or on the basis of a so-called general development of the human mind, but that on the contrary they originate in the material conditions of life [. . .]. The totality of these relations of production constitutes the economic *structure* of society, the real foundation, on which arises a legal and political *superstructure* and to which correspond definite forms of social consciousness. The mode of production of material life conditions the general process of social, political, and intellectual life [. . .]. At a certain stage of development, the material productive forces of society come into conflict with the existing relations of production or – this merely expresses the same thing in legal terms – with the property relations within the framework of which they have operated hitherto. From forms of development of the productive forces these [property] relations turn into their fetters. Then begins an era of social revolution. The changes in the economic foundation lead sooner or later to the transformation of the whole immense superstructure. In studying such transformations it is always necessary to distinguish between the material transformation of the economic conditions of production, which can be determined with the precision of natural science, and the legal, political, religious, artistic or philosophic – in short, *ideological* forms in which [*worin*] men become *conscious* of this conflict and *fight it out*.[29]

Now, besides the purely philological observation that refers to his *re-examination* of Hegelian legal philosophy as the determining factor in the methodological considerations recorded above, Marx certainly also means to make reference to the relevant *Contribution to the Critique of Hegel's Philosophy of Law* – as well as to the *Introduction to the*

Critique of Hegel's Philosophy of Law, published in 1844 and cited here. The *Critique*, as we know from the first section, is directly concerned with questions of logic and method. Apart from this one must point out, as part of the historical-systematic element, that the conception of method symbolized in the 1857 *Introduction* by the concrete-abstract-concrete circle allows us more than a strict and general *logical* view of the *structure-superstructure relation*. It also allows us to single out and define, in that *consciousness*, mentioned above at the end of the passage quoted from the *Preface*, the *decisive criterion* of *practice* as *moral* criterion, or criterion of *action*. This *closes* the circle by *verifying* the hypotheses, but is also an *intellectual* or technical criterion where the economico-social (etc.) *law* is proclaimed, into which the now-verified hypothesis is converted by practical experience, by action.

Marxists, Sweezy has stressed, are not only 'criticizing' the capitalist system, in that they have recognized its historical and hence transitory character. Rather, its critical, and hence its 'intellectual', position is also '*morally* relevant', as compared with a 'critical position regarding the *solar* system, whatever its imperfections'. It is also morally relevant 'since human *action* is itself *responsible* for the changes the *social* system experiences and will experience'.

Thus the *second thesis on Feuerbach* is clearly explained in all its methodologically revolutionary significance.

NOTES

1. Marx, *A Contribution to the Critique of Political Economy. Preface* (London: Lawrence and Wishart, 1971), p. 19.
2. Marx, *Grundrisse. Introduction* (translated by M. Nicolaus) (Harmondsworth: Penguin Books, 1973), pp. 85–6.
3. ibid., p. 87.
4. ibid.
5. ibid., p. 83.
6. ibid., p. 84.
7. ibid., p. 101.

8. ibid., p. 100.
9. ibid., p. 101.
10. ibid., p. 100.
11. ibid., p. 101.
12. ibid.
13. ibid., pp. 101–2. Della Volpe notes that a passage further on in Marx (after the quotation ending '. . . reproduces it as a concept in the mind') runs: 'the totality [of thought] is a product of the thinking mind, which appropriates the world in the only way possible for it' (cf. p. 497 of *Opere*, vol. 5 (Rome: Editori Riuniti, 1973)).
14. ibid., p. 102.
15. ibid., p. 103.
16. ibid., p. 104.
17. ibid., pp. 104–5.
18. ibid., p. 105 (the preceding quotation from Sweezy appears in his *The Theory of Capitalist Development* (London: Dobson, 1946), p. 31).
19. ibid., p. 107.
20. ibid., pp. 107–8.
21. The quotation is from Engels: cf. *Bol'shaya sovetskaya entsiklopediya* (2nd edn 1952) (Moscow), p. 270 (article on dialectics).
22. Introduction, op. cit., p. 106.
23. ibid., p. 107.
24. *Poverty of Philosophy*, op. cit., p. 174.
25. V. I. Lenin, *Materialism and Empirio-criticism* (*Collected Works*, vol. 14 (1908) (Moscow/London: Foreign Languages Publishing House/Lawrence and Wishart, 1962)), p. 143.
26. Marx, *Theses on Feuerbach* (*Collected Works*, vol. 5) (London: Lawrence and Wishart, 1976), p. 3.
27. Marx, *1844 Manuscripts*, op. cit., pp. 303–4.
28. A. A. Zhdanov, *On Literature, Music and Philosophy* ('On philosophy', 1947) (London: Lawrence and Wishart, 1950), p. 82.
29. Marx, *Preface*, op. cit., pp. 20–1.

INDEX